LETTERS ON
THE LEAGUE OF NATIONS

Supplementary Volume to *The Papers of Woodrow Wilson*

LETTERS ON
THE LEAGUE OF
NATIONS

FROM THE FILES
OF RAYMOND B. FOSDICK

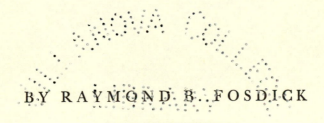

BY RAYMOND B. FOSDICK

PRINCETON, NEW JERSEY

PRINCETON UNIVERSITY PRESS

1966

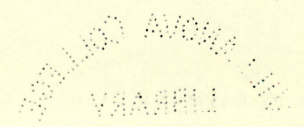

TO MY FRIENDS WHO ARE WORKING ON
THE PAPERS OF WOODROW WILSON
ARTHUR LINK, JOHN DAVIDSON, DAVID HIRST,
AND ALL THEIR ASSOCIATES
WITH ADMIRATION AND AFFECTION

FOREWORD

EACH GENERATION as Franklin Roosevelt said in 1936, has its rendezvous with destiny. History made large demands upon a generation of Americans in 1919 and 1920. Virtually the entire leadership of the United States had been preoccupied for more than two decades in domestic reconstruction and reform. Now, at the end of the First World War, these same men were thrust face to face with the realities of international life and asked to lead a world groping toward a new order and life.

The letters printed in this volume shed much new light on the reactions and responses of the most thoughtful, and therefore historically the most dynamic, segment of the American people in 1919-1920—that group of intellectuals who had furnished so much of the generative power for the progressive reformation at home. Except for a few in the very advanced guard, they had answered Wilson's call for a declaration of war against Germany in 1917 and had thrilled to his vision, described most vividly in his Fourteen Points Address, of a new world order. Indeed, they and their friends in Great Britain had given the President the liberal international program that he so eloquently synthesized and articulated.

The Treaty of Versailles—that mixed product of Wilsonian liberalism and European *Realpolitik*—turned hopeful expectations to ashes and noble dreams to nightmares for many young Anglo-American international liberals. Some of them, led by John Maynard Keynes in Great Britain and by Herbert Croly, Walter Lippmann, William C. Bullitt and Oswald Garrison Villard in the United States, turned in disgust and anger against the Treaty and its creation, the League of Nations. Among these Americans, at any rate, this reaction was not—as the letter from Walter Lippmann printed in this volume clearly shows—simply a matter of the disillusionment of the naïve. They thought that they could call the new world into being most speedily

vii

by forcing Europe to accept international liberalism as the price for continued American support of the peace settlement.

American liberal reaction to the Versailles Treaty has been interpreted heretofore almost exclusively through the men who demanded rejection of the Treaty. Actually, a majority of articulate American international liberals followed President Wilson, at least until January 1920, in pleading for ratification on the ground that the League of Nations under American leadership would bind up the wounds of the war and eventually rectify the injustices of the Versailles settlement.

The letters in this book vividly illustrate the dialectic between American liberals in the two camps in 1919-1920, and it is fitting that the chief spokesman of the Wilsonian liberals should be Raymond Blaine Fosdick. Born in Buffalo on June 9, 1883, he grew up in an educator's family, one that also produced Harry Emerson Fosdick, the great preacher and theologian. Transferring to Princeton in 1903 after two years at Colgate University, Raymond Fosdick at once fell under the spell of Woodrow Wilson, whom he later called "a scholar in action, a prophet touched by fire, with unmatched strength to persuade and move the hearts of his listeners." After being graduated with an A.B. in 1905, Dr. Fosdick stayed on for an additional year of graduate work at Princeton. He then studied law at the New York Law School and, like so many of his contemporaries, went into social work and municipal administration. He was one of Secretary of War Newton D. Baker's right-hand men during the mobilization on the Mexican border in 1916 and the war with Germany, and civilian aide to General Pershing in France in 1919. He was next President Wilson's own choice as the American who, as Under Secretary General of the League of Nations, should join two other young men, Sir Eric Drummond of Great Britain and Jean Monnet of France, in constructing the edifice of the new international organization.

Foreword

Dr. Fosdick's letters in this volume reflect his own hopes, dreams, and frustrations during the formative period of the League of Nations. Equally important, they reveal the intimate reactions of that group of American liberals who, having been thrust into the world at large, believed that it was within the power of reasonable men to bring good out of evil, order out of chaos. They are painful reminders of how the Treaty of Versailles was caught in the cross fire between the Senate and President, and of the growing despair among pro-League liberals occasioned by Wilson's refusal to compromise on the Senate's terms. Finally, they recall the dimensions of the tragedy that befell the world when a great leader was struck down and his forces were demoralized and scattered.

This volume marks the launching of a new series entitled "Supplementary Volumes to *The Papers of Woodrow Wilson.*" This series will consist of monographs, documentary volumes, and extended essays about President Wilson and his times, to be issued from time to time by Princeton University Press under the aegis of the Editors of *The Papers of Woodrow Wilson.* The Editors are happy to inaugurate this series with a volume taken from the papers of the greatest living Wilsonian and the man who gave leadership to the movement to edit and publish President Wilson's papers.

ARTHUR S. LINK
Edwards Professor of American
History and Editor of
The Papers of Woodrow Wilson

Princeton University
June 9, 1965

CONTENTS

Contents

Contents

LETTERS ON
THE LEAGUE OF NATIONS

THIS correspondence and letters to periodicals cover the period during which I served as Under Secretary General of the League of Nations (1919-1920); also included are a few letters relating to the League of Nations but written later. The original letters or the carbons of the letters which I wrote or which were written to me are now in my files which I shall ultimately give to Princeton University.

When I returned to America in May 1919, I had spent nearly six months with the American Expeditionary Force in France. Two days after I landed, Frank Polk, Acting Secretary of State, called me on the telephone from Washington to tell me that President Wilson, who was still in Paris, wanted me to accept the position of Under Secretary General in the League of Nations. Two or three days later, I had a cablegram from Colonel House in Paris, elaborating the idea. The other letters follow in due course.   R. B. F.

New York City
March 15, 1965

Letters on
The League of Nations

Paris   May 4, 1919

Colonel House to R. B. F. (cablegram)

At session of conference on April 28 after adopting League of Nations, Eric Drummond[1] was named as First Secretary General of League. He is a Liberal, was Secretary to Asquith and then Edward Grey[2] when he was Foreign Secretary. Since Grey's retirement he was Secretary to Balfour and held a most responsible position in the Foreign Office. A committee was also appointed by the conference for the purpose of drawing up organization plans for League. The committee made up one representative from U.S., Great Britain, France, Italy, Japan, Belgium, Brazil, Spain, and Greece. Committee will have their first meeting this coming week. It is planned that there shall be two Under Secretary Generals, one an American who shall be charged with duties of administrative and executive character. The other a Frenchman, whose duties will be diplomatic in character.

I very much hope you will permit me to suggest that you be designated as the American. You are, of course, familiar with the tremendous responsibilities with which the League of Nations is charged under the terms of the Covenant and by the Peace Treaty. It is absolutely necessary that we should have our very best men connected with organizing this great work and also that the men we select should be men of broad sympathies, thoroughly trained in big affairs and with liberal point of view. Geneva has been selected, as you know, as the seat of the League and the residences of the

[1] Sir James Eric Drummond, K.C.B., was a graduate of Eton who entered the Foreign Service. He served first as private secretary to Premier Asquith from 1912 to 1915, then to Sir Edward Grey until 1916, and finally to Foreign Secretary Lord Balfour. Drummond was appointed Secretary General of the League of Nations in 1918 and served until 1933. Later, as Lord Perth, he served as the British Ambassador to Rome.

[2] British Foreign Secretary at the beginning of World War I. Later, British Ambassador to Washington.

staff will be situated in the grounds that will be set apart for the officers of the League. During the coming summer most of the important work will be done, I believe, in London.

The expenses of the sitting under the terms of the Covenant are to be borne by the various members of the League and I am sure that the question of your salary will be entirely satisfactory to you. It is my opinion that there is no work in the world to be done at the moment more important than this work and I shall be personally deeply disappointed if you are unable to accept. I personally can assure you that I need your help in this great work. It is desirable, of course, that you should enter into your duties at once, but I think it could be arranged so that it would not be necessary for you to reach Europe before the first of July.

Sir Eric Drummond to State Department (cablegram)

London   May 16, 1919

Fosdick's acceptance is most gratifying. Please give him my sincerest thanks.

Colonel House to R. B. F. (cablegram)

Paris   May 31, 1919

See Julia Lathrop.[1]

1. Women should be represented on what League organizations or commissions?
2. What assistance can women and their organizations render in educating the people to the meaning of citizenship under the League?
3. Possibility of affiliation between the Secretariat of the League and women's organizations.
4. Possibility of establishing a women's branch as a section of the Secretariat.
5. Could Miss Lathrop come to London in July or August if necessary?

[1] Julia Lathrop was head of the Children's Bureau, Washington, D.C.

State Department to American Mission in Paris (cablegram)

Washington   June 1, 1919

Get interview by Drummond on the international character of the Secretariat and the need of setting up a framework to start things going immediately upon the ratification of peace. Fosdick is assisting provisionally in working out the tentative lines of organization.

R. B. F. to Colonel House (cablegram)

New York   June 24, 1919

Sorry to be a little delayed in arriving in London. Necessity of appearing before Congressional committees on War Department appropriation and of finishing up my work with the Commission on Training Camp Activities has made it impossible for me to get away before. Am sailing Saturday June 28 on *Aquitania*. Should arrive in London about July fourth or fifth.

State Department Press Release [I believe]

Washington   June 30, 1919

Raymond B. Fosdick sails shortly to take up his work with the provisional organization of the League of Nations. In this organization he will be one of two Under Secretaries General, Sir Eric Drummond being the Secretary General, and the three will constitute the Cabinet. Mr. Fosdick was appointed to this position by Sir Eric Drummond. The members of the permanent Secretariat are not to be regarded as representing any particular nation. The divergent interests of the particular States will be expressed in the Council and in the Assembly. The Secretariat is an international body and appointments are made without regard to questions of nationality.

Until the Treaty of Peace is signed and ratified, the League of Nations of course has no official existence. In case the League becomes an accomplished fact, however, it will be called upon to function almost immediately and a great deal of preliminary work is necessary. Ad interim appointments to the Secretariat will, of course, have to be subsequently ratified by the Council.

Memorandum to Sir Eric Drummond from R. B. F.

London   July 12, 1919

ADMISSION OF PRESS REPRESENTATIVES
TO MEETINGS OF THE COUNCIL OF THE LEAGUE

The question of the admission of the press to proceedings of the Council is, I believe, of critical importance, and its decision is fraught with wide-reaching consequences.

I.

If, as has been suggested, newspaper representatives are denied admission altogether, public confidence in the League will be destroyed at the start. Certainly this will be true in the United States. The decision to curtail the privileges of the press representatives at the Peace Conference in Paris, and to inform the public of the proceedings only through emasculated communiques did more than any other single factor to shake the confidence of the United States in the good faith of the peace negotiations and in the honesty of the treaty itself. The American people—the people of all democracies—are instinctively suspicious of public business conducted behind closed doors; and this suspicion has much to justify it. If the League succeeds, it will be because it has marshalled to its support forces which up to the present time have never been successfully mobilized. These forces consist largely of the faith and belief of common people, understanding and sharing in the plans and purposes of their leaders. If the proceedings of the Council are surrounded with secrecy, if the sole information given to the public is through a series of colorless and empty communiques, the confidence of the people in the sincerity of the enterprise will be

6

undermined. There is a new spirit at work in the world, resulting from all the forces that have been unloosed in the last four years, and the League cannot be guided in its decisions by old precedents. It is bound to take account of these fresh forces or it cannot survive.

The argument is advanced that this matter was fully considered in Paris and that it was agreed that there could be no freedom of discussion if representatives of the press were allowed to attend meetings of the Peace Conference. It is stated that so much leaked out of the Council of Ten that the Council of Four had to be established in its place, with rigorous precautions against publicity. To apply this analogy to the present case seems to beg the question. The analogy is based on the assumption that the decisions of the Council of Four were quicker decisions and better decisions than they would have been if publicity had been given to the discussions. This assumption is open to serious question. It is problematical whether a better peace might not have been evolved—a peace more calculated to endure—if the people of the world had really understood what was going on at the Peace Conference and had thus been able intelligently to place their support behind their leaders in the matters in which they were fundamentally interested.

But even if the argument be granted that more efficient results are obtained behind closed doors, it still remains to be considered whether, after all, slower decisions, or decisions that are perhaps embarrassed because they are shaped in the light of public opinion, may not be more than compensated by the confidence aroused by open and frank discussion. It seems to me that the same principle holds true here as in industry or government: that men are content with less efficient results provided the machinery and the instruments of control are in their own hands. It would be far better to go together and go slowly, even if the progress were not fast, than to court certain failure by engendering suspicion.

It is further said that if newspaper men are admitted to the meetings, the Council will at once be deprived of all reality, and the whole work will be done by private conferences outside. This may be true. It probably will be true at first until it becomes natural to discuss international matters in public, just as it became natural, after the adoption of the Federal Constitution in the United States, to discuss interstate matters in public. It is seriously to be doubted, however, whether the same formal type of meeting would not be evolved even with the newspaper representatives barred. The agenda of the Council will be carefully prepared, and I question whether, for some time at least, matters will be thrown into the Council which have not been fairly well considered in previous private conference. In other words, until representatives on the Council become accustomed to the frank and open exchange of opinion, and the world gets a sense of international solidarity, the formal character of the meetings is more or less inevitable.

II.

I am equally convinced that no compromise with the plan to open up the meetings to the representatives of the press, such as has been suggested in the proposal to have four members of the press assist in preparing the official communiques, would be acceptable. Certainly I do not believe that American press representatives would take part in such a scheme if it limited their right to present to their constituencies in their own words the proceedings of the Council. I am confident that it would be regarded as a bit of camouflage for the old regime, a sop thrown out to pacify the public. There is a principle at stake in this business which cannot be satisfied by the institution of halfway measures. . . .

R. B. F. to Walter Lippmann[1]

London   July 14, 1919

I have read with sympathy your articles, and those of Weyl's and Croly's, on the nature of the peace just concluded. It is an illiberal treaty from every standpoint, and there can be no hope of permanent peace under its auspices. Where I differ from the attitude of the *New Republic* is as to what should be done about the matter. You seem to think that the United States should limit its responsibility, and thus insulate itself against the consequences of the Treaty. Personally I do not believe that this is sound advice. The world is now so intimately bound together by economic and social ties that no nation can insulate itself. It is a sheer impossibility. We are all in this thing together to survive or perish, and while the Senate may seek to build some sort of barrier against future consequences, it can have no possible effect upon the world problem which confronts us.

I have therefore more or less resigned myself to the inevitableness of the present situation. The peace is made and signed, and I do not believe it can be unmade by the agencies that put it together. The hope of the situation—if there is any hope—lies in the League of Nations. Can the League, by the exercise of its somewhat vaguely defined powers, either now or in the future, so soften the sharp edges of the treaty that, by gradual transformation, it can be made the basis of enduring peace? That is the question that I constantly ask myself, and it was with the idea that I might help in answering it, that I accepted this post with the Secretariat of the League.

My reason for writing you is that I want your help—at least, I want your good advice, either now or at any future time. My question is this: How can the League humanize the Treaty? What practical steps, possible under the Covenant, can it take? I already have in mind four or five things

[1] Walter Lippmann was then an editorial writer for the *New York World*.

that might be done, in connection with the constitution of the Saar Valley Commission, for example, and with the selection of the High Commissioner for Danzig. These illustrations may seem trivial, but it is possible that they may prove an entering wedge, and that, given time and perspective and the possibility of future modifications, we can yet make the Treaty an instrument of lasting peace. My hope may be vain, but surely the attempt is worthwhile.

If in your study of this whole proposition, matters suggest themselves to you along this line, I would appreciate it tremendously if you would write me. I am extremely anxious that the permanent representatives on the Secretariat should keep in touch with the liberal forces of the world everywhere, and naturally I look to you and Croly and Weyl as speaking for the liberalism of America.

Walter Lippmann to R. B. F.

Whitestone, New York   August 15, 1919

I don't need to tell you how warmly I appreciate the point of view of your letter of July 14, and I want to write to you as frankly as you have written to me.

In my opinion the Treaty is not only illiberal and in bad faith, it is in the highest degree imprudent. It is a far worse job, I think, than the Treaty of Vienna a hundred years ago, because the men who gathered at Vienna did honestly take into account the balance of forces in Europe. The men at Paris ignored these forces. They have tried to make a world settlement on the basis of what seem to me three overwhelming fallacies. First, that the movement towards industrial democracy can be crushed. Second, that French diplomacy can be trusted with the mastery of the Continent. Third, that the power of America can be employed to maintain in status quo the impossible relationships created by the first two fallacies.

The reason that our group on the *New Republic* has urged the refusal of all material guarantees as to Europe is that we see at present no other way of restoring a decent perspective by Europeans on European affairs.

Let me illustrate. It looks now as if the bloody and immoral policy of counter-revolution in Russia has collapsed. Why has it collapsed? Fundamentally for two reasons. First, because there is no popular Russian support for Kolchak. Second, because the United States was unwilling to furnish the troops necessary for a successful conquest of Russia. The withdrawal of our aid has knocked the bottom out of the whole miserable plot and as a result we shall probably see within the next few months the conclusion of peace with Russia on terms that could have been obtained last February. This means simply that the true balance of forces reasserts itself.

Now I believe that France under this treaty is pursuing a policy in Central Europe and Western Germany which is not only immoral but impossible without the American guarantee, and I am convinced that once we serve notice that we are not a pawn in M. Pichon's[1] game, France's common sense will begin to reassert itself.

So much in explanation. You ask how can the League humanize the treaty. A month ago I was still trying to believe that it might. I don't think I believe it any longer. So far as the League is concerned on the Continent it is today a bureau of the French Foreign Office, acting as a somewhat vague alliance of the Great Powers against the influence and the liberty of the people who live between the Rhine and the Pacific Ocean. Owing to the unanimity clause and particularly owing to the constitution of the Council and the new triple alliance within it, the League will be what the French Government and the British Government make it. They were able at the Peace Conference to defeat the President at every vital point. Under these covenants they will be far more effective than they were at the Conference, and while something may be accomplished by putting good men on various commissions, we have to remem-

[1] Stéphen Pichon, Minister of Foreign Affairs in Clemenceau's cabinet.

ber that in the business of preventing future war there is small credit in almost having prevented it.

We have to wait for a complete change in attitude within England and France. When this occurs we have to insist on the inclusion of Russia and Germany in the Council of the League, and only then shall we be able to say that a League of Nations is possible. Whether such a League will be the evolution of this one or something created after this one has collapsed, I don't know. But I am certain that the present League is in structure and function and ideal the enemy of a real League of Nations, and the greatest danger is that its failure, like that of the Holy Alliance before it, will disillusionize a whole generation.

You ask for my suggestions and I give them to you in the spirit you ask them. The first necessity is that the President, and if not he then Colonel House, should permit the whole world to know just what the dangers of this settlement are. An American should have done and should still do what General Smuts[2] did. Until that primary act of honesty is committed we shall be living a lie and committing one immorality to cover another. The plain fact is that nobody can get away with this Treaty, and the sooner that is confessed so that all the world knows it, the better for the world. There is no mystical power whatever in this covenant. It consists of a group of governments, and the error which it seems to me affects certain liberals today is their enormous desire to believe that the covenant is greater than the Great Powers. It would be if there were any popular representation in it, but that has been rigorously excluded. I think if I were in your position I should make publicity my whole aim. I should try to arrange the procedure so that no matter what the immediate cost the world can understand the real forces at work.

[2] A South African statesman and soldier. Strong supporter of Woodrow Wilson and the League of Nations at the Treaty of Versailles. He warned against "a scramble among the victors for the loot."

Memorandum to Sir Eric Drummond from R. B. F.

London   July 30, 1919

To Sir Eric Drummond: Here are some tests or standards to measure the growth of the League in the direction we want it to go.   R. B. F.

TESTS OF THE LEAGUE

1. Mandates which shall not be cloaks for annexation.
2. Publication of them before final acceptance, in order that discussion may be provoked, as in the case of the Covenant.
3. Publicity to meetings of the Council and the Assembly.
4. Appointment of impartial persons as chairmen of the Saar Valley Government Commission, and of the Danzig Commission.
5. Early meeting of the Assembly.
6. Consideration at such an early meeting of the question of admission of Germany to the League, the question of disarmament, and the question of conscription.
7. Character of the Permanent Court of International Justice.
8. The League to keep scrupulously clear from assuming any duties assigned by the Treaty to the Principal Allied and Associated Powers.
9. Consideration by the Executive Council at an early meeting, of the Anglo-American-French Treaty, and discussion at which publicity shall be given as to whether it is or is not consonant with the Covenant of the League.

Memorandum to Sir Eric Drummond from R. B. F.

London   July 30, 1919

THE FIRST MEETING OF THE ASSEMBLY

Reasons advanced for postponing the first meeting of the Assembly:

1. The impossibility of adequately preparing the items of the agenda, as, for example, the details of the Permanent Court of International Justice, the Transit Convention and the Health Convention.
2. Necessity of having a satisfactory meeting of the first Assembly, so that thereafter the meetings will attract responsible statesmen, i.e. Prime Ministers, Foreign Secretaries, etc.
3. Impossibility of securing consent to admit Germany if meeting is held at an early date.
4. Desirability of allowing an interval between Paris sessions and first meeting of the Assembly so that men who have been engaged in the former can have a vacation.
5. The calling of the Labor Conference in October makes it unnecessary to call the Assembly until later.
6. Desirability of having interval between Labor Conference and Assembly meetings.

ARGUMENTS AGAINST POSTPONEMENT

I.

It seems to me that there is a bigger and broader view to take of the situation than that suggested by the arguments above noted. The League is a *family* of nations. It represents nations large and small around the world. It is natural, therefore, that in creating a new method of association, the *family* should get together for common counsel. It is the most auspicious way in which to start the enterprise. Great perils have been faced and unexampled hardships shared in common, and to avoid such perils and hardships in the future, the nations of the world meet together. Discussion and an open exchange of opinion will provide an atmosphere and create a spirit in which the details of common action can more effectively be worked out.

Without such a meeting at an early date, the League will take on the aspect of an alliance between those few powers represented on the Executive Council. The first

14

meetings of the Council will attract the attention and publicity of the world, and the suspicion will tend to spread among the neutral powers and the smaller nations that the League holds nothing for them. If there is a long interval between these Council meetings and the meeting of the Assembly, this suspicion will harden into conviction, and the meeting of the Assembly, when it is finally called, will appear nothing but a sop thrown out to satisfy the lesser states.

On the other hand, if the Assembly is summoned at an early date, it will give tangible reality to the existence of the League as a family of nations. It will be the visible sign of a new hope in the world; and in the economic perils that face us this coming winter, it will constitute a factor of stability.

The economic situation of the world is indeed perhaps the most vital reason for calling the Assembly as early as possible. By October many of the Powers, for reasons of self-protection, will doubtless be engaged in various kinds of discriminatory practices as regards commercial relations. We shall be face to face with the most serious economic situation that has ever confronted us. If, in the midst of this common peril, representatives of all the nations get together for common counsel, much can be done to clear the air and allay suspicion and distrust. If the meeting is allowed to lie over until this suspicion and distrust are more or less crystallized in the shape of rigid discriminatory commercial treaties and practices, the task of bringing order into the world will be almost hopeless.

II.

In this connection the special situation of America offers abundant reason for an early meeting of the Assembly. My country has hardly been touched by the war. Compared with the losses of England and France, her losses are trifling. She has gold and raw materials in abundance. Her commercial facilities are unimpaired, and the whole world is her debtor. The existing rates of exchange are but an evidence of her unique prosperity. Already there are indications that she intends to maintain this advantage. This determination shows itself, for example, in the conditions which she apparently intends to impose upon the extension of her credit to Europe; and I am not a little fearful of pre-war commercial practices and regulations, backed, perhaps, by tariff enactments and shipping legislation, by which she will attempt to solidify her position.

If, at an early date, before the situation assumes a rigid form, a meeting of the Assembly could be held in Washington, representing the need and public opinion of the world, I believe that much could be done to bring home to America the fact that the interests of Europe are *her* interests. America is isolated from European public opinion. She really does not understand the economic chaos which the war has brought about. If this could be clearly portrayed to her in her own Capitol, it would, I believe, serve to retouch and revivify the tremendous idealism with which America entered the war in 1917, and again awaken a realization of her kinship with the fate of Europe. The meeting would attract the widest publicity throughout the country, and if the situation were properly handled by the representatives of European Powers, it would do much to break down the isolation of America and put her immediately in touch with the currents of European feeling. It is important, however, as I have pointed out, that this should be done at an *early* date, before the idealism of 1917 and 1918 wanes, and conditions crystallize under the touch of material prosperity.

III.

It is more important at this juncture that the world should have concrete evidence of solidarity and cohesiveness than that it should continue in its old ways of suspicion and jealousy while its leaders discuss the details of plans for common action. The man in the street cares little about the machinery of the Court of International Justice or about transit conventions or any of the other details of coopera- tion. He is thinking of food and coal and the possibili- ties of making ends meet. Even though the Assembly can provide him with none of these things, the symbolism of a great international gathering will supply that promise of a better fortune which will help him to cope with the diffi- culties of the present. It is for *him* that the Assembly should be called at an early date.

I am perfectly willing to admit the possibility that nothing very concrete or tangible will grow out of the first meeting of the Assembly. I believe, however, that deliberate thought would disclose a number of things for the Assembly to do, even at a meeting in October, and that an agenda worthy of the event could be produced. But that is not entirely the point. The point is that the world should be made to realize in a vivid way that it is a family, that the interests of one are the interests of all, and that the Assembly con- stitutes a mechanism through which forces can be set in operation to guard against common perils.

R. B. F. to Mrs. Raymond Fosdick

London   July 31, 1919

We eat and sleep in terms of the League's present status and future development. And of course we do a lot of speculating on how soon it will become a really effective instrument. Yesterday Drummond, in something of a philo- sophical mood, was inclined to stress the *inevitability* of the League. That is, he feels that with the fast developing interdependence of the world as an economic unit, time is running on our side, and the sheer necessities of the situation will force the growth of some kind of world or- ganization, even if we were to muff this particular attempt. Monnet[1] and I were inclined to qualify this point of

[1] At the age of thirty, Jean Monnet was head of the French supply organization in London. He was appointed by Sir Eric Drummond as

view. We do not feel that time is running on our side, except in the sense of a future too remote to be of advantage to this generation or to the next. This generation is in a race with international anarchy, and Monnet and I stressed the point that the world has very little time in which to set up the framework of international government and *establish the habit of teamwork*. We have far too little time to do a good job before the strains and stresses come. And the danger—the really frightening danger—is that before the nations have learned how to play ball together, they will be overwhelmed by some new emergency —like a football team that has to meet its strongest opponent at the beginning of the season when it is only half-trained.

That is why it seems to us that the present job is so urgent —so immediately compelling—and of course Drummond agrees completely with this. It was a grand debate.

R. B. F. to Frank Polk[1]

London   August 12, 1919

I am only too glad to have Whitney Shepardson[2] in Paris with you, and I know that in keeping in touch with your office, he can be most useful to us both. The other day you suggested that you could provide him with accommodations at the Crillon. The League will provide for his travelling expenses and such other incidental expenses as he may have, exclusive of room and board, so that between us, I think we

---

Under Secretary General of the League of Nations in 1919 and served until 1923.

[1] A New York lawyer, appointed by Secretary Lansing as Assistant Secretary of State. At this time, Polk was Acting Head of the American Peace Delegation in Paris.

[2] A Rhodes scholar, Mr. Shepardson was a member of the American Peace Delegation in Paris, where he served as an assistant to Colonel House. At the Colonel's suggestion, he became my assistant when the Secretariat was setting up its preliminary offices at Sunderland House in London. He served from 1918 to 1919 and was succeeded by Captain Gilchrist. Subsequently Shepardson became one of the main organizers of the Council on Foreign Relations.

can take good care of him. I shall be over myself within ten days, and hope to be able to have a confab with you on many matters.

R. B. F. to Newton Baker[1]

London   August 15, 1919

Any letter from you is a delight, but a letter in your own handwriting is a privilege. Yes, the world is moving, and we are on the threshold of great developments. Your letter encourages me to put down on paper some of the ideas which have been running through my head during these past weeks. They are the result of a pretty intense preoccupation with League affairs and of many talks with House, Cecil,[2] Drummond and others. I am putting them down—for what they may be worth—more as a means of clarifying my own thinking than of enlightening you.

1. Whatever we may wish, out of loyalty to the President, to think about the Treaty, parts of it are definitely bad, notably the Reparations Section, the Saar Valley and Upper Silesian settlements, the Shantung business and probably the Polish Corridor. Nothing but trouble can come out of these decisions; they are not and cannot be permanent settlements. I do not say that anything better could have been obtained at Paris. From everything I can hear, the President staged a gallant battle against the representatives of countries whose war wounds were far deeper than ours and whose point of view necessarily could not be as objective and detached. I have little patience with those who criticize the President because he was unsuccessful in obtaining more concessions. And I have less patience with those who attack France and Belgium and England because they insisted on

---

[1] While serving as Mayor of Cleveland, Ohio, Mr. Baker was appointed Secretary of War by President Wilson in 1916 and served until the end of the Wilson administration in 1921.

[2] A descendant of a distinguished family in England, Lord Robert was attached to the British delegation at the Treaty of Versailles. He was a strong supporter of Woodrow Wilson at the Peace Conference, and won the Nobel Peace Prize in 1937.

harsh terms. If we had gone through what they went through, our demand for a vindictive peace would have been just as determined—and just as unwise.

2. In spite of the fact that the President didn't like it—at least so I am informed—Smuts' valedictory at Paris represents the only sane view of the Treaty as a whole that anybody can hold. Without the League of Nations, the Treaty by itself is hopeless. With the League of Nations we have an opportunity—a promising opportunity—not only to work our way out of the ruin wrought by the war, but to establish a new standard and a new technique in international relations.

3. In his Metropolitan Opera House speech the President said that the Treaty and the League were so interwoven that they could never be dissected. This may be true in the sense in which the President meant it, but in another sense it is not true. I have recently made a pretty careful study of the distinction in terms of responsibility which the Treaty makes between the League on the one hand and the Allied and Associated Powers on the other, and I am relieved to discover that the enforcement of the harsher measures is in the hands of the latter body and not the former. For example, the League has nothing to do with the Reparations Commission or with the demarcation of frontiers, except for the Saar Basin, or with the control of German rivers or with the supervision of the military demobilization of Germany. These matters are all left to the Allied and Associated Powers. It is true that the League must appoint a High Commissioner in Danzig and thus assume some responsibility for the Corridor question; and it is true, too, that we are tied in—regrettably tied in—to the administration of the Saar Valley until the plebiscite 15 years from now. But by and large, it is the organization of the Allied and Associated Powers that bears the brunt of trying to enforce the more unfortunate sections of the Treaty.

4. It seems to me that this is a great advantage to the League. It relieves us of a responsibility which would break

down all our attempts to bring a new order and a new spirit into the affairs of Europe and the world. If the League succeeds it will be because its emphasis has been positive and creative, rather than repressive.

5. I realize, of course, the danger of this situation. There will be *two* organizations in the world—the League and the Allied and Associated Powers, and I foresee over the next year or two a discouraging period when the League perhaps will be overshadowed by a more authoritative and potent agency. Certainly it will be a more dramatic agency. But this seems to me unavoidable, and in the end, considering our position today, desirable. For the Allied and Associated Powers will be up against an impossible job that cannot be worked, while the League will be slowly building a standard for just and fair dealing to which the sanity of mankind will ultimately respond. In the end, I believe the League will liquidate the wreck of the Allied and Associated Powers and we can then start off in the spirit of the Covenant.

There are plenty of people over here who would like to have the League now assume responsibility for the Reparations Commission and the other punitive measures. But this, it seems to me, would be a ghastly mistake. Let's steer clear of these things and give ourselves time to establish our work in the confidence and conscience of the world. The League stands for disarmanent, for peace, for international justice, for the protection of backward peoples, for a better standard of living, for the relief of suffering, for the fight against disease. Let's stick to that program and let the other crowd see where they get with theirs. They'll fail at it, because the future belongs to men with new creative ideas and not to men whose eyes are bloodshot from the past.

6. The non-political activities of the League are going to be immensely important and are going to furnish an admirable place to start the building of a new technique. I mean the functions outlined in Articles 23 and 24 of the Covenant—the control of disease, drugs, traffic in women

and children, arms, communication and transit, etc. The world has had far too little practice in international activity. To be sure we've had the Universal Postal Union and the International Bureau of Weights and Measures and the International Sugar Commission, and during the war we had the successful operation of such cooperative ventures as the Allied Maritime Transport Council. But we never had a systematic international approach to problems where everybody has everything to gain and nothing to lose. And it is going to be an excellent practice field for the sterner problems that await us in the future. Through these relatively non-controversial matters we can build a technique; we can establish a procedure and develop precedents; we can get the "feel" of international cooperation in pursuit of a common goal. Each step that we take, however halting, every decision that we reach as a result of frank discussion, will be a definite advance toward ultimate world peace. The result will be that when another Sarajevo comes, the world can meet it with a system which has been developed and matured in many different areas and in many meetings of the family of nations.

7. Too little attention has been given to Article 19 in regard to the responsibility of the League to conditions which are outgrown and therefore no longer applicable. Cecil tells me that this Article as originally drafted was part of Article 10 and that its purpose was to prevent the use of Article 10 as a means of maintaining the status quo. He thinks it is more important than Article 10 and I most emphatically agree. The arrangements of the world must be capable of continuous revision. Otherwise solidification sets in and we run the risk of trying to work with forms and ideas which once were satisfactory but which have long outlived their usefulness. It is because of this process of crystallization that explosions occur.

8. An early meeting of the Assembly is of vital importance. This, rather than the Council, is ultimately bound to be

the influential body of the League, and the dramatic effect of having all the nations of the world sitting around a table in common council on problems that face the human race, regardless of boundary lines, is going to be tremendous. The very symbol will tend to develop a unity among nations that nothing else could do. It will do for the world what the first Continental Congress did for the thirteen colonies not only in providing a means of effective collaboration against common perils, but in introducing a consciousness of unity and of the ties that bind separated groups together. There is a disposition in some quarters to shelve the first meeting of the Assembly to some distant date, and allow the Council, which is dominated, of course, by the great powers, to make all the initial decisions. But it seems to me that from every point of view this would be a mistake.

9. The Secretariat of the League is, or at least can become, one of its most vital parts. As you know, it is fashioned on the pattern of the British permanent civil service. It is the eyes and the ears of the League—the branch that never adjourns and that is always in session—collecting facts, analyzing data, submitting its recommendations to the Council and the Assembly. Its attitude is, and of necessity must be, wholly impersonal. Its members must be divorced from their allegiance to their respective governments. They serve only the League. If this idea seems novel, think how strange it must have been to our forefathers in 1787 to have a New Yorker or a Virginian attached to the Federal Government without any allegiance to his own state.

Of course the Secretariat will be successful only as it commands the services of the ablest minds available, regardless of nationality. So far we are experimenting. None of us is trained for the job. My own training is perhaps less adequate than that of the others. But we mustn't hesitate to change the personnel as better men are found.

A standard of excellence must be maintained, and this applies to everybody from the Secretary General down to the messenger at the door.

R. B. F. to Dr. Abraham Flexner[1]

London   July 15, 1919

Some proposals have been made looking to the establishment of an educational branch or bureau of the League of Nations, and I would very much like to get your advice and help on this matter. I enclose herewith a note by H. A. L. Fisher,[2] addressed to Lord Robert Cecil, together with comments thereon by Headlam-Morley,[3] of the British Foreign Office, and Mr. Pym, member of the Secretariat of the British War Cabinet, who sat at Paris during the Conference.

My own idea is that, instead of the League of Nations going out definitely to form an educational branch, we should give encouragement to the creation of some international body which would be independent of our control and would administer its own affairs as it saw fit. With this body, the League should establish a close liaison arrangement and perhaps by advice and counsels, direct them into the right channels. The thing that I am anxious to avoid is a topheavy and cumbersome machinery here in the League of Nations. If everybody who has an idea is allowed to take it to the League in the shape of a definite branch or bureau, it will not be long before the machinery of the League will be impossible to run, and we shall be so entangled in incidental matters that the main business of the League will be forgotten.

It occurs to me that the National Education Association, at its meeting a week or two ago, may have taken some

[1] Flexner at this time was Secretary of the General Education Board, founded by John D. Rockefeller, Sr.

[2] An English historian who supported Woodrow Wilson.

[3] He was a strong British supporter of Woodrow Wilson, and wrote *Studies in Diplomatic History*, published in 1930.

action on this matter looking toward the creation of an international educational body. Do you know whether they did anything along this line, and if they did, do you suppose you could get me a copy of their minutes or proceedings?

If you have time, would you mind dictating to your fair Mrs. Bailey just what you think of all this business, what an international educational body would do, how it would function, and just what its relationship to the League of Nations should be? This is all new ground for me, and naturally I turn to the source of all wisdom in educational matters.

The work here is opening most auspiciously, although we are still in a state of more or less chaos, struggling with plans and theories, and embarrassed, of course, by the fact that we really do not exist. It is the first time that I have ever been attached to an organization that had no corporeal existence, and the doubt as to whether we shall have such an existence does not afford much of a basis for definite future plans.

Dr. Abraham Flexner to R. B. F.

New York   August 14, 1919

I have read and—as I have walked in the deep forests of Scarsdale—pondered the weighty educational problems upon which you consult the oracle. Here are my conclusions offered for what they may be worth:

1. Cecil's suggestion of an educational annex to the League is to my thinking, to say the least, premature. The League will be overburdened with immediate practical problems connected with and resulting from the peace treaties. It will be difficult for its executives to find and direct a competent personnel. The League, as an organization, and the officers, as individuals, will have to win the confidence of the largest menagerie of quarreling and unregenerate animals ever brought together in one circus. Is success in this task easy or assured? Far from it. Will

success be made easier or more assured, the more things the League attempts? On the contrary, every additional job it essays adds possibilities of failure, miscarriage and friction. Education is of slow growth. There's nothing urgent about it even in the Balkans. The difference between starting something now and starting something—even assuming something is feasible—a year or two hence will in the end be negligible. The whole League proposition is in danger of being "too scopy." The closer you fellows keep to earth, to concrete, insistent, manageable problems, and the further you can keep from local interference in other matters, the more likely you are to accomplish something. In your place I should—as I see it—oppose needless or avoidable extension of function or increase of personnel as likely to impair efficiency, to make trouble or to invite failure at this point or that. Hence, my vote on Cecil's proposition, would be "postpone without prejudice." For the present, I should not even consider your compromise, viz., forming an outside international body connected with the League by a liaison arrangement. I'd stop, look and listen for a while and see whether the thing can make good on its immediate tasks.

2. Fisher's two suggestions seem to me to emanate from British perplexities rather than from an objective study of either the general situation or the Balkan situation. The "conflicting claims of education and industry" are on the carpet in England and perhaps one or two other nations; are they so in Servia or Greece? I should be sorry to see the League select the objects of its educational activities—if such there come to be—on the basis of off-hand suggestions, obviously arising from the vexatious troubles of a particular minister. The same can be said of Fisher's suggestion about foreign students. England wants foreigners to study at its universities and wants Britishers to go abroad. Ergo, let the League of Nations run a Cook's agency for students! Nothing to it! The situation as respects England and the situation as respects Turkey or Servia can't be met

by the same piece of machinery. Students from America and France will go to England just as they got to going to Germany—when there is enough to go for and when the conditions are such that it is readily available. No amount of boosting or machinery will do the trick otherwise. On the other hand, the backward nations in Eastern Europe need in education what they need in industry and sanitation—guidance at home, guidance that keeps in touch with local needs, resources, possibilities, history, etc. The Rockefeller Foundation can help Servia, for example, more effectually by lending the Servian Government an educational adviser, if he's the right man, than any piece of administrative machinery run by Englishmen and Frenchmen at Geneva, and relying on circulars, conferences and all the other familiar devices. So much for Fisher.

3. Headlam-Morley's comment is, as I understand it, in favor of "hands off." But his reason does not seem to me sound. "Education to be effective should express the most vital indigenous moral and intellectual sentiments of the nation. The international is often superficial," etc. Isn't this British to the core? Of course, no one supposes that educational systems can be transplanted without adaptation; but cannot one nation learn from another in matters of educational policy and procedure? Our system of medical education is better than the English or French because we have learned from both England and Germany and adapted the hints to American conditions; we have made quicker progress than England or France in our graduate schools, because we have learned from Germany, adapting the hints to our conditions, while the English and French are still "indigenous." If Mr. Headlam-Morley will read Matthew Arnold's report on Secondary Education in Germany made in 1868 and ponder Arnold's recommendations, or Michael Sadler's book on Continuation Schools, he will see that in education one need not be wholly indigenous—and had better not be. But the League of Nations, just being born, isn't a promising agent of international educa-

tional suggestion and initiative—I agree with Morley as to that.

4. Pym's suggestions overleap machinery and propose to make the League at once a direct educational agency, if, as I assume, he means the League is to interest itself in his specific suggestions or things like them. Pym is right that everything desirable and attainable depends in the last resort on education, but it doesn't follow that the League would be wise to undertake to be *an* or *the* international educational dynamo. He's surely wise in leaving it "to others to devise the necessary administrative measures." Pass the buck! The N.E.A. did nothing, as far as I know, bearing on this subject. Concerted action may become wise or necessary, but let things quiet down first. Before you fellows act, get some facts about definite needs and possibilities—don't go off half-cocked.

The League had better, for the present, stick to jobs it can't escape, instead of going after jobs of questionable appropriateness. Cecil made that suggestion, not because he saw something educational the League *had* to take hold of, but because it occurred to him that no League could be complete if education were unrepresented. It's all the difference between having something to do and having to do something.

R. B. F. to Dr. Flexner

London   August 30, 1919

Your fine letter on education and the League arrived the day after I wrote you a saucy letter inquiring why you had not replied.

We all enjoyed your letter very much. By "we" I mean Sir Eric Drummond and others of my colleagues who share my secrets on all sorts of matters. Your memorandum really will help the situation very much over here, in that it helps to clear the air as regards a lot of vague vaporing on the question of education.

I shall write you more about it as the situation develops.

P. S. The enclosed editorial may interest you. I sympathize especially with its point that gents engaged in political work (like me, for example) should be free from the sordid cares of earning an income.

Memorandum to John D. Rockefeller, Jr.,[1] from R. B. F.

September 4, 1919

This memorandum does not assume to cover the compelling moral reasons why America should join with the rest of the world in a brotherhood of nations, or should accept her share of responsibility in keeping order in backward countries. It does not attempt to meet the various points urged against the Covenant in the United States. It merely undertakes to set forth a few of the practical conditions which seem to make America's participation in events beyond her own borders a sheer necessity if the world is to be preserved from chaos.

1. It is a truism that economic rivalries constitute the basis of all wars. America is now setting out to maintain the commercial advantages which the exigencies of the last five years have given her. The entire world is tremendously in her debt, and her own facilities, both in terms of finances and manpower, are unimpaired. The condition of industrial underproduction which exists everywhere in Europe as a result of war paralysis, has scarcely touched her. She is developing her merchant marine to an extent not dreamed of five years ago, and is rapidly assuming a position where she can dispute with England the supremacy of the seas, while in the Pacific she has only Japan for a rival. This situation is viewed in Europe and particularly in England with the utmost apprehension, and already the question is being asked whether Great Britain must maintain a sizeable navy against America, as she maintained one against Germany. For it must be remembered that navies are the

---

1 Only son of a well-known father, he devoted his life to philanthropy.

indispensable adjuncts of competing merchant marines. Without some definitized system of international relationships, therefore, such as a League of Nations would provide, this growing economic rivalry is bound to be accentuated both by tariff discriminations and trade agreements by which each of the contending parties will try to promote its own affairs to the disadvantage of the other.

History is full of examples of just such struggles, and they lead to but one thing—war. Every great international industrial rivalry in the world, both ancient and modern, has led to this goal: Rome and Carthage, England and Spain, England and Holland, France and England, and lastly in this great catastrophe through which we have just passed, England and Germany.

Already there are signs that trade discriminations are being practiced and that international jealousies are being aroused. Unless these discriminations and jealousies can be controlled through the instrumentality of a League, we shall hand on to a succeeding generation a bloodier war than that through which we have just come.

2. International industrial antagonism as the basis of misunderstanding and disagreement is nowhere better illustrated than in the situation which is developing now in regard to the coal problem. In 1913, for example, Great Britain was producing 292,000,000 tons of coal annually. In 1919 it is estimated that she will produce but 62 per cent of her 1913 output—in other words, 183,000,000 tons. This leaves but a small margin over and above her own domestic consumption, so that instead of exporting approximately 100,000,000 tons a year as she did before the war, she will actually export but a small percentage of this amount. Which of the countries that in normal times depended upon this export margin is to get it? Already Italy, France and Belgium are bidding for it, and it is an open secret that at least one of these countries is willing to pay for it not only its cash price but in terms of preferential tariff agreements with Great Britain. So that we have in this single arrangement alone the

possibility of trade contracts between two countries which would discriminate against the rest of the world.

But to continue the example of the British export of coal: production of coal in England today is in effect under a government subsidy. Great Britain therefore takes the position that while she will sell coal at the pithead for domestic consumption at one price, such coal as is exported must sell at a far higher pithead price in order to cover, if possible, the cost of the subsidy. Consequently, whoever gets England's surplus margin of coal, whether it is Italy, France, Belgium, or all three, must pay a price for it which will make it impossible for the industries of those countries to compete on an even footing with similar industries in England. Those countries therefore will be face to face with the loss of their foreign markets, while as regards their own domestic market they will be obliged to set up tariff schedules against the import of England's industries, insofar as they compete with their own, equal to the difference between what English manufacturers and their own pay for coal. Moreover, as a retaliation for their losses they will doubtless discriminate against England in the export of those commodities which England particularly needs.

This is but a single illustration of a situation which will be multiplied everywhere if there is no coordinating organization of nations through which trade rivalries can be so regulated as to prevent unfair and discriminatory practices. If such an agency is not immediately instituted, not only will the world revert to the conditions that existed prior to the war, but those conditions will be greatly intensified by reason of the fact that the competition for raw materials and food, due to the shortages that everywhere exist, will be keener than ever before.

This last point is of very great importance. With margins of coal and raw materials as low as they are at present, a single country has it in its power to prevent the resumption of production by other States, and thus cut off the economic recuperation of its rivals. It is inevitable that such situations will lead to international bitterness and eventually to war. A nation will fight before it consents to starve. If the economic stability of the world is to be maintained, the principle must be established, as Mr. Hoover has pointed out, that there are certain foundations of industry, such as ships, railways, waterways, coal and iron, which no matter what the national or personal ownership or control may be, partake of the nature of public utilities in the use and enjoyment of which other nations have a moral right.

In this whole plan to re-establish the world's industry, it is impossible for America to keep aloof. She is as intimately bound to the fate of Europe in everything that relates to industrial prosperity or chaos, as New York is bound to California. The world is now inextricably enmeshed in a single industrial net. No laws which Congress can pass can isolate the United States. Underproduction in England or France, or a trade war between Italy and Czecho-Slovakia will have its repercussions in every state of the Union.

3. I said in my first paragraph that the entire world is tremendously in America's debt. The figures of this debt are staggering and are reflected in rates of exchange that have cut the pound to 85 per cent of its former purchasing value in terms of the dollar, and the franc to 40 per cent of its former value. This is a condition which affects America as unhappily as it affects Europe. In Europe it means that a premium of from 15 to 60 per cent is added to the cost of all goods imported from America. It means that an Englishman must pay 1s.2d. for every shilling's worth of produce which comes from the United States, while in France, the Frenchman pays approximately 2 francs for every franc's worth of imported commodity. This situation is a double-edged sword. It amounts practically to a high tariff wall erected against the import of American goods, thus raising prices to European consumers, while on the other hand America's export trade is declining because Europeans simply cannot afford to buy American commodities. The industrial well-being of the United States depends upon the continuance of our export trade.

The only solution of this situation, of course, lies in a stream of exports from European countries. This involves, first, the re-establishment of the industries in Europe which the war has wrecked, and, second, an influx of raw materials for which in large measure Europe looks to America. Thus we have a vicious circle: Europe unable to buy in America because of an upset exchange, and yet unable to balance the exchange because of a lack of raw materials which she must buy in America.

There is just one thing that can correct this situation and that is credit. Credit is the priming of the pump. America must extend her credit to Europe on a generous basis, so that the wheels of Europe's industry can be started and the flow of commerce back and forth across the Atlantic can be renewed. On what are these credits to be secured? Who is going to guarantee them? How can they be arranged? Who is going to undertake to supply those countries which need abnormally long credits? Who is going to lay out the plan by which all needy countries will be aided on a common basis, and not merely those whose securities appear most satisfactory? Finally and most important, who is going to guarantee a condition of order in Europe without which credits cannot be extended, or, if extended, would be rendered worthless?

There is but one answer to these questions. We must have an agency representing the nations of the world in the preservation of order and in the settlement of international problems, under whose jurisdiction and through whose machinery an Economic Council can work out the bases upon which the industry and trade of the world can be uniformly re-established.

4. Another problem which confronts the world and which can be solved only through international action, is the problem of debased and inflated currency. The disappearance of gold as a medium of exchange, the topsy turvy values of currency in such countries as Poland and Czecho-Slovakia, the tremendous amount of clever counterfeiting,

particularly of German marks, which the Bolsheviks have carried on, have produced a chaos which can be solved only by international counsel. Moreover, during the war, many countries have raised funds by the simple expedient of issuing paper money, a practice which is now bringing home its burden of trouble, not only in the countries in which it has been carried on, but in other countries bound by commercial ties. Under the auspices of a family of nations, an International Currency Commission could be appointed to diagnose the situation and provide the remedy.

5. So far, I have been speaking largely of the industrial conditions which seem to establish conclusively the need of a League of all Nations. There are political reasons which are just as compelling and which point even more conclusively to the necessity of America's participation in helping to maintain the burden of right international relations. America has no axe to grind in this whole business; her disinterestedness is above suspicion. She is the one great Power in the world whose participation in the settlement of Europe and Asia can create no distrust. When the Poles realized that a plebiscite in Upper Silesia would be difficult to hold in an honest fashion without the presence of troops, it was American troops that they asked for. When the Armenian question came before the Council of Four, it was America who was asked to take the mandate. When the troublesome problem of Constantinople was discussed, again it was America who was asked to assume responsibility for managing the affairs of the city and district on an equitable basis. In establishing the personnel of the various boundary and administrative Commissions set up under the Treaty, it is to the United States that the Powers are looking for men of unbiased judgment. Indeed, one gets the impression that American disinterestedness can save the world in this whole situation, and that without America there is no solution.

6. The Treaty of Versailles together with the Covenant was necessarily a compromise between conflicting national

interests. Nobody is satisfied with the arrangement as it stands—neither the extremists, whose sole idea was punitive as against Germany, nor the idealists, who hoped that out of the negotiations would come a permanent solution based on equity and justice. Whatever may be thought of the Treaty, it is the proposed Covenant of the League that can save the situation. Article 19 of the Covenant, which places upon the Assembly the responsibility of advising the reconsideration of treaties that have become inapplicable, and of conditions whose continuance may endanger the peace of the world, is the foundation upon which great changes can be built. The League as created is far from perfect, but it is a *beginning*, and with it as an instrument, there is hope—indeed it is this generation's only hope—that order can be built into the world and that justice and fair dealing can be established as the permanent basis of international relations.

Memorandum to Sir Eric Drummond from R. B. F.

London   September 6, 1919

I have just had an hour's confidential talk with a representative of the London *Times*, who came to see me with a personal letter. I am greatly disturbed by what he tells me. He is recently back from the Saar Valley and he says that the French Military Command is carrying on in a quiet sort of way a series of deportations and is putting into operation a boycott, designed to rid the country of the Germans. He further says that German public officials are being removed and that the policy is identical with that pursued by Germany in connection with Alsace-Lorraine after 1871. He states that this is being done quietly so as not to disturb Paris, and that whenever Paris seems to show an interest in the situation, the thing is soft-pedaled, only to be resumed when Paris thinks of something else. He, of course, cannot write anything about it in the *Times* because of the fear of upsetting Anglo-French relations, but he thought we ought to know about it.

He gave me equally disturbing information about our Civilian Commission on the left bank of the Rhine. I understand that there is a Commission of Four consisting of a Frenchman, an Englishman, an American and a Belgian. The Chairman is a Frenchman and has the power of casting an extra vote in case of a tie. The American and the Englishman seem to be playing together, while the Frenchman is making up to the Belgian, with the result that the votes are generally three to two. Apparently the policy of the majority of this Commission is to rid the left bank of the Rhine of "disturbing elements."

This situation seems to me to be one of extreme seriousness. Have you any information on this proposition?

> *Drummond's endorsement*: No, and I am equally perturbed. The only remedy for it is the appt. of the governing Commission with a non-French chairman and I doubt whether we shall secure this unless at the meeting of the Council, when the question is discussed, an American representative with full authority is present. The dilemma is obvious and I see no solution. As regards 2 the best chance seems to me to be publicity.   E. D. 9/6/19

R. B. F. to Frank Polk

London   September 8, 1919

I am enclosing herewith for your confidential information a memorandum by C.J.B. Hurst[1] addressed to Mr. Balfour, dealing with the French attitude toward the mandates for Togoland and the Cameroons. A copy of this memorandum came into Drummond's hands and he suggested that I show it to Colonel House. I talked with the Colonel last night about it down in Withyham, and he asked me to send a copy of it to you.

Personally, I do not believe that the remarks made in the Supreme Council meeting of May 7th can possibly support the hypothesis that Togoland and the Cameroons are not

---

[1] Judge of the Court of International Justice at The Hague (1924-1936).

to be subject to a mandate. Certainly, the President in his cablegram to Colonel House and in his later cablegram to you, does not concede that anything was agreed to in the Supreme Council which would constitute so obvious a violation of the letter and spirit of the Covenant. I have not myself seen the minutes of the meeting of the Supreme Council for May 7th, but from what Drummond tells me, based on his recollection of them, the President is right in his contention. That is, the conversation had to do with *exceptions* that might be made in these territories in connection with the raising of black troops and did not at all affect the question whether or not the territory should be taken under mandate.

I think, therefore, that while granting everything that the unfortunate conversation of May 7th seems to imply, we can justify the position that both the Cameroons and Togoland will have to be taken under a mandate—a "B" mandate for the Cameroons, and either a "B" or "C" mandate for Togoland. The character of the Togoland mandate is a detail which can be arranged in due course. In regard to the exceptions about the raising of black troops which the meeting of May 7th seems to have made possible, Drummond tells me that Clemenceau made the remark in this meeting that he had nothing more in mind than a *volunteer* army. Drummond's suggestion is, therefore, that the French should be held to this remark in granting the exceptions to the mandates; at least it could be used as a factor of trading because a volunteer army in the Cameroons and Togoland is precisely what the French do not want.

As I say, I have not the minutes before me so that I cannot argue precisely to the point on this matter. There are still two or three questions that should be cleared up, which can only be cleared up by someone who is in position to see the minutes: first, should the exception in regard to black troops apply also to the Cameroons? The President obviously does not think so. Drummond thinks that it would be difficult to eliminate the Cameroons from the application of this exception. Second (as noted above) should Togoland have a "B" or "C" mandate?

Colonel House will arrive in Paris next Saturday and I know you will want to talk with him about this matter.

P.S. I would suggest that you show this to Shepardson.

R. B. F. to Arthur Sweetser (cablegram)

London   September 11, 1919

There has been no intention at any time to appoint Butler[1] as Director of the International Labor Office. He has been Secretary of the Organization Committee of the Labor Conference and it was suggested that he act as Secretary of the Labor Conference in Washington until the Director was appointed. Director should be a Labor man and inasmuch as the Secretary General of the League is an Englishman, the Director of the Labor organization should belong to another nationality. Drummond heartily concurs with this view. The two objections to Butler therefore are first that he is an Englishman and second that he is not a Labor man. Shotwell is not a Labor man and I do not believe he would have the support of labor in the United States. I am confident that no action has been taken which will prejudice the free choice of Director.

Memorandum to Sir Eric Drummond from R. B. F.

London   September 22, 1919

I talked this morning with Benjamin Strong, Governor of the Federal Reserve Board of New York, about my economic memorandum of September 4th. While agreeing with most of it, he took certain exceptions:

1.   He agreed that economic rivalries constitute the basis of most wars, but thought that racial antipathies had a good deal to do with them too.

---

[1] A member of the British Civil Service. He became deputy director of the International Labor Office under Albert Thomas.

2. He thought that technically it might not be true that the world was tremendously in America's debt, because of the vast bank deposits of foreign countries in the banks of New York. These deposits perhaps amount to two billion dollars, and have been placed there because America, due to the rates of exchange, is really the financial center of the world. This, however, is a technical and perhaps temporary objection.

3. Strong emphasizes the point that it is not going to be possible to control economic rivalries except insofar as they are the result of political action. Favored nation clauses can probably be eliminated and discriminatory tariffs against particular countries to serve particular ends can doubtless too be done away with in time; but rivalries which result from the free exchange of commodities, that is, the free flow of trade, cannot wisely be interfered with by the League except when they are promoted by governments for political purposes. For example, if the German government said to the Krupps that it was very necessary to capture the market in steel rails in America, and that it, the German government, would pay a large bonus upon armament orders placed at Krupps if the latter would reduce the price of steel rails in America to a certain minimum— this would constitute a trade agreement for political purposes which doubtless the League could control. On the other hand, it would be obviously impossible for the League to ask Chile to reduce its export tariff on nitrate—a tariff which operates against the whole world. This tariff pertains only to Chile and has nothing to do with trade discriminations. So that all the way through my memorandum, Strong would insert the idea of *the political use of trade rivalries.*

4. Strong is inclined to believe that Hoover's idea, mentioned on page three, is wrong, inasmuch as it involves inherently the violation of sovereignty. Personally, I believe that while we may not be able to get this idea through in

the present state of the world's thinking, it is certainly an ideal to hope for.

5. Strong thought that my sentence about the industrial well-being of the United States depending upon the continuance of our export trade, was in part fallacious although he admitted that it was an idea that was everywhere preached and that it was the basis of all our tariff legislation. He contended that there could be no such thing as one-sided trade—that is, that exports must be matched by imports, or there is no trade, and exports without imports defeat themselves. He condemned strongly our whole tariff legislation on the theory that it was built around the idea of discriminating against imports and stimulating exports. He said that the effect of our tariff legislation was inevitably to raise prices for the poor man. This is proved, he said, by the present situation in England where the unbalanced exchange practically amounts to a tariff wall against imports, with resulting high prices. The rich are not affected because they can afford to pay for such luxuries as break over this tariff wall, while the real effect of the whole business is to raise the price of such necessities as are imported, with only the poor really suffering.

6. He objected to my expression that America had no axe to grind in this whole business. He said that she had no *political* axe to grind, which places her in a unique situation as regards other countries; that she has several commercial axes to grind, however, is obvious. Strong, as I said above, believes in the unimpeded flow of trade and doesn't think that the League has any mission to interfere with industrial rivalries except those which are political in nature. For that reason he thinks that Article 19 of the Covenant is pretty weak, inasmuch as the conditions whose continuance endangers the peace of the world are largely industrial conditions. They are not conditions which the League will have any effect in changing.

Sir Eric Drummond's Official Appointment of R. B. F. to the Labour Conference

London   October 3, 1919

In view of the labour sections of the Peace Treaty, especially Articles VI, XII and XIII, and of the fact that the Labour Conference is held under the auspices of the League of Nations, it seems to me desirable that certain members of the International Secretariat should go to Washington for the purpose of attending the meetings of the Conference.

The Secretary General of the League of Nations may be required to give assistance to the International Labour Office,[1] and, as I am not able to go myself, I have asked Mr. Fosdick to attend as my personal representative. He will have full authority to act on my behalf. I have also requested Monsieur Varlez,[2] as Director of our Labour Section, to proceed to Washington.

It is desirable that as close a liaison as possible shall be formed between the International Secretariat and the Labour Office. No doubt this will be much helped by personal contact at the early stages, and the duties of the members of the International Secretariat who attend the Labour Conference should be to give their assistance to the Labour Secretariat etc. in any way which may be required. I feel sure that they will realise that it would be very undesirable for any appearance to be given that the International Secretariat of the League of Nations was endeavouring to interfere in any way with the policy, conduct or administration of the Labour Office or of the Labour Conference. The position will, I fear, be one of some delicacy but I know that Mr. Butler thoroughly appreciates the situation.

[1] The International Labor Office (I.L.O.) was established by the Treaty of Versailles. It represented a progressive step in the relationship between owners and workers, and the original idea was that this attitude toward labor would be adopted by all the nations in the League.

[2] Belgian citizen who became head, temporarily, of the Labor Section of the Secretariat of the League of Nations.

On all questions in which the Secretary General is concerned, Mr. Fosdick will, of course, take decisions, and, as regards technical labour matters, Monsieur Varlez will, no doubt, act in consultation with him.

Sir Eric Drummond to R. B. F.

London   October 10, 1919

I think it well that when you go to America you should be fully informed of the position of the very difficult question arising under Article 393 of the Treaty as to which are the members of chief industrial importance. You will see the general description of the problem from the copy of a statement received from the Organising Committee of the Labour Conference which I am enclosing herewith.

The letter from M. Lafontaine[1] states that "it is of great importance that the question which are the eight States of chief industrial importance should be settled before the Washington Conference meets, so that the Government Delegates of the remaining countries at the Conference may proceed to select the four other members who are to appoint to the Governing Body."

This will in any case be impossible as the Council will not be meeting before the date fixed for the opening of the Labour Conference. It would, however, serve the purpose in question if a decision were given before the Conference closes, and unless agreement is previously reached we shall have to make an attempt to secure this.

Time will, however, be very short as it is highly undesirable that the question should be put before the Council before America has ratified, and with no American therefore present at the Council (even if there is a meeting of the Council before the American ratification) .

The general description of the position in the document forwarded from M. Lafontaine shews the great difficulties

[1] Henri Lafontaine was President of the Council of Administration of the mines of the Saar Valley, under Clemenceau.

which will be experienced in arriving at a formal decision of a judicial character, and it would of course be extremely convenient if it proved possible to arrive at an agreed settlement without formal reference to the Council.

The legal position under the Article appears to be that the duty of the Council to decide only arises on an appeal after an earlier failure to agree. The Treaty does not, however, clearly allocate responsibility for making the initial decision for which appeal to the Council is so provided. It does not appear to assign this duty (or to give this power) either to the Organising Committee or to the Conference, and the responsibility would therefore appear to rest directly upon the several Governments to attempt to agree in the first instance. The members of the Organising Committee would, however, seem to be a natural channel for the Governments to use in carrying out this duty, and I am not in anyway suggesting that the members of that Committee have gone outside their proper province in taking the action they have. All I wish to convey is that in doing so they have been a channel by which the several Governments have been attempting to carry out a responsibility resting directly on themselves under the Treaty rather than as a body specifically carrying out a duty assigned to them by the Treaty itself. The importance of this is that the suggestions they have made for a list do not preclude a further discussion of the question by representatives of the different Governments before the question is formally considered by the Council.

It may prove possible to take advantage of the presence of the representatives of different countries at Washington to arrive at such an agreement, and if so, this would be desirable from every point of view. Any such agreement would, on the interpretation of the Clause indicated above, be an agreement of the several Governments through their representatives and not formally a decision of the Conference as such. It might be well if you were able to inform the President of the Conference unofficially of what we believe to be the correct legal view, as he may feel it advisable in the circumstances to rule out of order any discussion of the subject by the Conference on the ground that a decision does not legally fall within its competence.

Perhaps you would take steps at the earliest possible moment on your arrival to see whether such a settlement is possible. In going into the question you should bear in mind the fact that claims for inclusion in the list of eight have been received from Canada, Poland, Sweden and India. It is important that the representatives of these countries as well as of those on the original list should be a party to any agreement, otherwise the question will of course be left for settlement by the Council.

You will of course realise the importance of informing us at the earliest possible moment whether such a settlement is possible, or whether the question must go forward for decision by the Council. It would be well for this purpose to cable to me at least a fortnight before the date at which it is expected the Labour Conference will terminate, and if possible the notice should be longer.

Will you please shew this letter to Varlez and perhaps you would discuss it with Butler.

> *In accordance with instructions from Sir Eric Drummond, I sailed for New York on October 8, 1919. My headquarters were in Washington, D.C., and I remained there until March 1920, when I returned to London to finish up my work with the League.*

R. B. F.

R. B. F. to his Family

Washington   October 23, 1919

Over everything in Washington hangs the shadow of the President's illness. The lines of Walt Whitman's poem keep running through my head: "where on the deck my captain lies." And truly the ship is without a captain, and its precious cargo of hopes for a saner world is in dreadful jeopardy.

R. B. F. to Mrs. Raymond Fosdick

Washington   October 24, 1919

After nearly a year's absence, the atmosphere of Washington seems strangely different. Of course it was obvious in 1917 and 1918 that the Republicans didn't like Wilson and I shall always remember how T.R. (it was at that private dinner in New York) referred to the President as "the gray skunk"; but T.R. was never given to understatement about his political opponents. Anyway, the Republican dislike of Wilson here in Washington has changed to open hatred. In spite of the fact that he is a desperately sick man, they still hate him, and the comments you hear at the capitol or in the hotel lobbies are almost unbelievable. To hear people talk, you would think that Wilson was the chief enemy of his country. It is dreadful to come back from Europe where his name is revered and find this vitriolic feeling at home.

R. B. F. to Colonel House

Washington   October 23, 1919

I have been thinking over (Lord) Grey's proposal that due to the illness of the President the meeting of the Assembly should be held in Europe, and I am more than ever convinced that your decision in this matter is absolutely right. Three months will intervene before any possible meeting of the Assembly can be held, and the President has an excellent chance of recovery. Even more important, it seems to me, is the necessity of giving the United States a visual impression of the League. International conferences have always been held in far away places like The Hague, and we do not know what they look like or feel like. Even if the President were not able to preside, and Mr. Lansing or someone else had to take his place, the presence in America of such men as Clemenceau, Lloyd George, Lord Robert Cecil, and others, would put the League on the map for those who still believe that Europe is only half-hearted in its support.

I know I do not have to argue all this to you, but as I thought of the matter coming down on the train yesterday, it seemed especially important that the plans for holding the Assembly in Washington should not under any circumstances be altered. Europe can have the Council meeting, but let us have what is going to be the real epoch making event—the first meeting of the Assembly.

Colonel House to R. B. F.

New York   October 24, 1919

Thank you for your letter of October 23rd. I am glad you still hold to the opinion which we both expressed when you were here concerning the meeting of the Assembly in Washington.

By the way, Beer[1] tells me that you never took up with him the memorandum which I gave you from Mr. Lansing regarding Mandates and other matters. I have no copy of this and I would greatly appreciate it if you would return it as soon as possible.

When do you expect to be in New York again?

Memorandum Prepared by Arthur Sweetser,[1] Manley Hudson,[2] and R. B. F.*

November 1, 1919

THE SENATE RESERVATIONS FROM THE EUROPEAN STANDPOINT

The United States today stands at the Rubicon. The Democrats and the Republicans face each other in deadlock,

---

[1] George Beer was chosen to head the Mandates Section of the League of Nations, but died before he could take office.

[1] A graduate of Harvard, Mr. Sweetser entered journalism. After serving briefly with the *New Republic*, he became the Associated Press representative in Germany and advanced with Von Kluck's dash on Paris in 1914. Later he was Associated Press correspondent covering the

the former refusing to accept the Peace Treaty with the reservations proposed by the latter, the latter refusing to accept any compromise proposed by the former. The parliamentary situation is drifting desperately towards an impasse from which there will be no outlet. In this crisis it is a positive duty of American citizenship to consider the probable results.

There is one new and almost neglected phase to the situation. That is the attitude of the rest of the world outside our own frontiers. Strangely enough, we have almost entirely neglected it so far. In an extreme desire to safeguard American interests, as we express it, we have gone forward with utter disregard of the reaction of that group of States upon whose side we fought in the war, and of that still larger group of States with whom we must continue to live in the future.

Let no one think that the reservations proposed in the Senate are mere words, that in a short time they will be forgotten and the League will go on unaffected. There is only too obvious a willingness in America to consider the Senate situation simply a battle of legal experts and politicians. On the contrary, the reservations proposed are both revolutionary and positive. If we allow them to pass in a happy-go-lucky spirit on the ground that after all they are not much more than verbiage, let us realize in advance that the world outside will not be so carelessly minded.

State Department. In 1918, he was appointed a member of the American Peace Commission in Paris, where he served as an assistant to Ray Stannard Baker, who headed the American Information Service. Sweetser was appointed to the Secretariat of the League of Nations in 1919 and served until 1941. Thereafter he served as an official of the United Nations under Trygve Lie.

2 Professor of law at Harvard University and for a few months after 1919, connected with the Secretariat of the League of Nations.

* This memorandum was drawn up by the three of us with the idea of expressing frankly our feelings about the reservations proposed by the Senate. What we chiefly had in mind was to get the American people to understand how the European nations felt about them. Of course, we wrote the memorandum anonymously, for we were all connected with the Secretariat.

One of our easy American customs is to pass a law about something which troubles us—not with any idea of enforcing it rigidly, but to have it handy in case of necessity. This custom is not understood abroad. If we ask reservations which we may not intend to use, we have no right to expect the world to bind itself in the same lighthearted way. One vital demand of the present situation is that we look upon these reservations with the same realistic viewpoint with which those nations whom we ask to accept them will in their turn look upon them. We must not, as many earnest people still do, consider that because we may not invoke the power of these reservations, the other nations of the world can, in justice to themselves, do anything else except examine them in their most cold-blooded, legal interpretation. Whether or not we use the special privileges which we demand, those privileges nevertheless remain to be called upon at any moment of crisis.

The immediate result of the passage of the sweeping reservations proposed would be another prolonged delay in the re-establishment of peace and the ending of the war restrictions. No nation could for a moment be expected to agree to bind itself to these reservations without a very detailed and elaborate analysis of all the possibilities which they create. Inasmuch as they give us a position of peculiar advantage in the League, the other Powers will undoubtedly face a long period of uncertainty as to whether they should accept or reject them. They will hesitate to reject them. They will hesitate to reject the reservations, because rejection would mean a League of Nations without the United States. On the other hand, they would hesitate to accept them because they would not willingly handicap themselves in an agreement in which all Powers should stand as equals.

We would, therefore, continue in a state of war perhaps for several months more. Our relations with Germany and the liquidation of our war problems would remain unsettled. The resumption of our trade and commerce with Germany would largely be left to the decision of England, France,

Italy and Japan, for we could make no real move until they acted. Our position would rest absolutely in their hands.

We could not cut this knot by a direct declaration of peace with Germany. The situation is far too complicated for that. The speediest course of action open to us would be to draw up a wholly new treaty legalizing all the steps we had taken in the war, such as the seizure of enemy ships and property, and restoring the shattered mechanism of trade. Even if we were to take over bodily certain sections of the present treaty already dealing with these subjects, the mere work of preparing for, drafting, and signing a new treaty would consume months of time.

The effect of further delay upon Europe is beyond calculation. As Mr. Hoover has pointed out, every day lost adds to the menace of the future in those war-torn lands. "The powder magazines of Europe cannot be destroyed until this Treaty is ratified," he says, "and during every day of delay more explosives are being poured into them." We cannot regard the well-being of Europe as of no concern for us or take a course of action deliberately calculated to threaten it.

More serious than the delay would be the practical certainty that the other nations, if they accept our reservations, would feel bound to make counterreservations in their own protection. It is preposterous for us to think that we can enter the League of Nations on a specially privileged basis, free of many of the obligations binding other nations, or that these other nations have no particular points and principles which they too would desire to have excluded from the operation of the League, once this policy of national self-seeking prevailed.

It may not be generally known that in England, France and other countries reservations have been vigorously pressed for the protection of specific national interests. Strong forces in Great Britain have urged the exclusion of Britain's naval supremacy from League action. Equally strong forces in France have demanded the disregard of the world's judgment on the Rhine provinces. Italy is even now torn by internal strife to make the Adriatic a domestic issue. Powerful interests in Switzerland are endeavoring to except that government from the clauses relating to economic compulsion. Poland, Czecho Slovakia, Roumania and Jugo Slavia would undoubtedly seek to except themselves from the clauses relating to the treatment of minorities, clauses which present perhaps the most substantial, ethical gain of the Paris Peace Conference.

If the United States makes a reservation, for instance, allowing it to increase its armament at its own good pleasure, what possibility is there that we shall ever bring about the gradual disarmament of nations, for which this war was largely fought? If we push on to reserve the broadest kind of questions as within our domestic jurisdiction, what right have we to protest if France makes a similar reservation for the German Rhineland, or Italy for the Adriatic? Once we get into that sort of thing, there is no end to the upcropping of selfish exceptions which the militarist and reactionary forces in all nations are only too anxious to make.

The drastic reservations of the Senate would establish the precedent for a competition of reservations which would tear the whole tissue of the League into shreds. We could not refuse other countries what we demand for ourselves, and if we assume that we have no higher duty than to look after our own interests, we cannot deny the same assumption to other Powers. With this spirit operating, there would be left nothing but the shadow of the League which the United States had given the world the right to expect, and all the complex and complicated work done in Paris, when each nation was brought to make concessions in the interests of all, would be wiped entirely off the boards. If there is to be a family of nations to maintain the peace of the world, there must be a certain minimum of confidence and fair play.

All this, however, is based on the assumption that the other nations will find some way to accept our reservations.

That assumption, however, is extremely dangerous. To one who has been closely associated with the situation in England and France, it is extremely doubtful if the foreign governments will agree to be bound by them. They will not knowingly sit down to a game in which the cards are stacked against them, or in which the United States is allowed to hold several aces up its sleeve. They will not willingly consent to enter a compact where one of the parties asks them to agree that it will not assume any responsibilities except such as from time to time it may choose.

Rather than enter into such a one-sided bargain, it seems dangerously probable to one who has been closely connected with the situation at Paris, London and Washington, that the powers will decline to accept America's membership.

High Japanese authorities, whom it is not possible to quote by name, have stated that while Japan might have acquiesced in the reservations if no positive acceptance were required of her, she could not possibly acquiesce in them through the formal exchange of notes demanded. This viewpoint is perfectly understandable because the Shantung reservation, justified though it is, is very decidedly a criticism of that whole settlement which represents Japan's prime stake in the war.

The British are known, also from high authority, to be very reluctant to enter a League of Nations where the advantage is all on our side. Moreover, their close relations with Japan would make it extremely embarrassing for them to have to go to the length of writing a note of positive concurrence in the Shantung reservation.

The French and Italian view, while not so definitely expressed, may be said to point to very serious consideration of the necessity of getting on without the United States. The reaction of the French is only too well shown in a series of editorials just received here, of which the following are examples:

MATIN November tenth: "The reservations mean that the United States can withdraw from the League of Nations whenever it pleases and be the sole judge as to whether it has fulfilled the obligations foreseen by the Covenant. The Society of Nations appears no longer to exist. It can live only if the most powerful nations accept rules in common. The Treaty created the obligation for all countries not to leave the society without two years' notice which is no longer valid for the American Senate. If the United States makes the application of the treaty dependent upon the acceptance of reservations which destroy its bearing, is there any Peace Treaty left?"

ECHO DE PARIS November ninth: "The Republican majority seems to have recovered its vigor when it came to the reservations. The result of these is to free America from all obligations relative to the pact of the League of Nations. Let us have no illusions; reservations discredit the League of Nations."

There now arises the possibility of a League of Nations without the United States. Both French and British statesmen have said that those two countries are so firmly pledged to the League idea that they will carry it out whether we join or not. Undoubtedly that is their spirit and intention.

We cannot, however, deny that they will not be able to construct a League of Nations, in the sense in which the world has come to use the word, without the participation of this country.

This fact arises from no virtue of ours. It is due entirely to our geographical situation. Located as we are, largely apart from the rest of the world, we are able to be disinterested in most of the world's explosive problems and can therefore serve somewhat as a balance wheel. The United States as a member of the League would be recognized as a great impartial outside influence, able to steady and stabilize the course of the whole organization.

If we do not go into the League, it is possible that the neutral States will, in turn, refuse to enter, and the League will deteriorate into a perpetuation of the old war alliance. Many neutral states are now openly awaiting the action of the United States before making their decision. Swiss spokes-men especially have stated that Switzerland will not join a League without the United States, because our absence would mean that the League would be merely a renewal of the Entente group, which for some time would not be strong enough to take Germany and Austria into its organization.

This difficulty is a very real one for the Entente powers. With the United States a member, they could afford to admit Germany and Austria, as their own ideals and purposes would still retain the preponderance of strength within the League. If, however, the United States were not a member they might easily be confronted by a situation in which Germany and Austria in a restricted league could out-manouver them.

Let no American for a minute think that he can unchain all these possibilities upon the world without at some time paying the penalty. Whether we like it or not, it is a fact that we have stirred up new hopes and aspirations among the peoples of the world; that we have helped to elevate the standards of statesmanship and diplomacy; and that we have given the world the right to expect of us something better and finer than it has known before. This is no light responsibility; it is, on the other hand, a great obligation and a great opportunity.

Americans must realize that it was the United States, practically unaided at the start, that drove through the con-cept of a better international cooperation. We raised that banner when we went into the war; we went forward with a battle cry wholly new to the diplomacy of Europe; we saved what we could of idealism out of a badly battered peace conference. It is not mere phraseology. It is, on the other hand, the sternest and harshest kind of fact, that the world looks to the United States for inspiration and guidance.

It is still more a stern and harsh fact that during the recent weeks we have practically shattered that attitude. Europe stands amazed before the fact that the nation which it had accepted as a leader towards a better world-organization, is now the only nation which is in fact jeopardizing that organization in every way. People in Europe are utterly bewildered at the doubts and hesitations, the charges and recriminations which they see arising from this side of the water. They wonder if, during all those days of the war they were wandering in a dream when they followed the American leadership for a League of Nations, or whether now our present attitude does not show that we were at that time grossly hypocritical and insincere. The world has no conception of our interior politics, nor indeed of our traditional policies. All it knows is that the nation which has battled the concept of a League of Nations through every difficulty to final success is the nation which now, at the last moment, without warning, threatens to torpedo it.

R. B. F. to the Secretary of War

Washington   November 7, 1919

I am wondering if you will be good enough to read the memorandum which I am enclosing on the fourteen reservations to the Treaty now pending before the Senate. Now that I have written this, I do not know what to do with it. The State Department has a copy, and I have sent a copy to the League to Enforce Peace. Have you any suggestion as to where it might be effectively used? I have felt that it was best not to have my name used in connection with it, inasmuch as my relation to the League might be misconstrued on the Hill.

R. B. F. to Colonel House

Washington   November 7, 1919

I am enclosing a memorandum on the fourteen reservations to the Treaty now pending before the Senate, which Hudson, Sweetser and I jointly prepared. Now that we have gotten it out of our systems, we don't know exactly what to do with it. I have sent a copy to Mr. Lansing and another one to Secretary Baker in the hope that if there is any merit in it at all, they can put it to some effective use. Of course, we have done it anonymously because we didn't want League officials to be visibly connected with it. I think it might be well to get a copy into the hands of the people at the League to Enforce Peace.

The news here in Washington is pretty depressing and it begins to look as if the situation in the Senate would result in an absolute deadlock, in which the Democrats might be forced to defeat the Treaty. The Republicans are determined to jam through their reservations without change, and without positive leadership on our side the situation is none too hopeful.

However, by the time this reaches you, some change may have occurred.

R. B. F. to Sir Eric Drummond

Washington   November 7, 1919

The situation in the Senate has changed so from day to day that I have hesitated to write you about it for fear that before the time my letter reached you an entirely new phase of the drama would be on the boards. The drama as it is now being played is partly a tragedy and partly a farce. It is a tragedy because the Senate does not realize with what colossal stakes it is playing in its attempt to humiliate the President. It is a farce because it is as flagrant an exhibition of small politics as we have ever had in the Capitol.

Today things look as critical as they have at any time, and it begins to appear very doubtful whether the Senate is going to avoid the deadlock which seems inevitable. The reservations which are now being discussed vitiate our entire adherence to the Covenant, and I do not see how they could possibly be accepted by any other Power. Personally, if these reservations go through, I do not believe I would care to serve as an official of the League, because it would place me in the impossible position of participating in an attempt to induce other members of the League to fulfill the terms of the Covenant, when my own nation had announced in advance our intention not to fulfill them....

The President's illness leaves us without leadership on our side, and taking full advantage of the situation, Senator Lodge and his cohorts have run away with the game.

This is pretty disturbing news, I know, and I would not write it at all except for the fact that if the situation changes you will know of it by cable before this letter reaches you. At the present time, as I say, we are living through depressing times.

R. B. F. to Sir Eric Drummond

Washington   November 7, 1919

You will remember that we talked over the system of universal military training which the Secretary of War is advocating here in Washington. I have had several talks with Secretary Baker about the matter, and I told him that liberal opinion in Europe was considerably disturbed at this new attitude on the part of the United States. He has just completed an article for the "Manchester Guardian," which by the time this reaches you, may have been published. I am venturing to enclose a copy of it herewith. I confess that while he makes an excellent case, I am not entirely convinced. General Pershing has recently recommended to Congress a substantial reduction in the 500,000 men army which the Secretary has proposed, and while some form of universal military training may be adopted, I doubt if the particular plan that the Secretary has in mind will come through. My interest in this, as you know, is entirely its effect on the disarmament plans of Europe. I should hate very much to see any scheme of ours over here used as an excuse for large armaments on the Continent.

R. B. F. to Gordon Auchincloss[1]

Washington　November 11, 1919

I am sending you herewith a memorandum which Hudson, Sweetser and I jointly prepared, dealing with the Treaty Reservations. I sent a copy of it to Colonel House, and a copy has gone to the State Department. I don't know that anything will come of it, but we hated to sit by and see the League done to death, as it is being done down here in Washington. Needless to say, it is an anonymous contribution. It is possible that the League to Enforce Peace will print it.

The State Department is asleep at the switch, and I confess I do not feel at all hopeful about the outcome of this situation.

Memorandum to Alexander Kirk[1] from R. B. F.

New York　November 11, 1919

Mr. Sweetser told me this morning that in a conversation with you on Saturday or Sunday, you expressed your surprise that I was sending messages to Sunderland House through the channel of the British Embassy rather than through the State Department. There appears to be so much confusion and misunderstanding about this business, that as a matter of record I want to set down the details of the whole story.

I sailed from England on October eighth. Before I left, I asked Mr. Butler Wright[2] at our Embassy in London if he would be good enough to expedite messages which Captain

[1] He married a daughter of Colonel House and was his assistant in the negotiations leading up to the Treaty of Versailles.

[1] Mr. Kirk was assigned as secretary of the Legation at The Hague in February 1917. In 1919, he was assigned as assistant to Secretary of State Lansing at the Paris Peace Conference, following which he returned to duty in the State Department.

[2] In 1912, Wright became Consul General to Roumania, Servia, and Bulgaria. He was made Counselor of Embassy at Petrograd in 1916 and had the same title in London in 1918.

Gilchrist,[3] my assistant, might have occasion to send me. As I was not certain whether this arrangement would be acceptable to the State Department, I made a similar request to our Military Attaché, so that in the event that one channel broke down, I should not be without some official means of communication. My intention was to take it up with both the State Department and the War Department as soon as I arrived in Washington, to determine what channels would be desirable. In addition, Sir Eric Drummond, at my request, arranged with the British Foreign Office so that I could use that means of communication in case of necessity.

A day or two after my arrival in America, while I was still in New York, Sir Eric Drummond sent me a cablegram. Apparently he gave the cablegram to Captain Gilchrist to despatch, for it came over the military wires. General Churchill sent a copy of it to me, and apparently sent another copy to the State Department. The fact that the military wires were used seemed to cause the State Department considerable distress. I heard about it from two or three quarters, and Colonel House, in New York, suggested that I take it up immediately with the State Department and straighten out any misapprehensions that might have developed.

When I came to Washington, therefore, on October 22, I saw you at your office. You felt that it would be far more fitting to use the State Department as a channel of communication, and expressed your belief that such a method would be approved. You said that you would take it up with Mr. Lansing. That very afternoon, having occasion to cable to London, and not knowing whether I could use State Depart-

[3] A graduate of Williams who obtained his Ph.D. at Columbia, Huntington Gilchrist entered the Army in 1917. When I needed two men for service in the Secretariat of the League of Nations, I asked General Pershing in Paris to select two capable officers. He strongly recommended Captain Gilchrist and Lieutenant Howard Huston. We put Huston in as the Establishment Officer of the Secretariat, and Gilchrist became my assistant. He served on the Secretariat for nine years. Later he served as American minister to Belgium (Marshall Plan) and as United Nations representative in Pakistan.

ment facilities, I sent a message to Sir Eric Drummond through the British Embassy. On October 27th Mr. Chris Herter,[4] of your office, telephoned in my absence and talked with my secretary, Miss Wisherd. He made the request that all official messages in connection with the League of Nations be sent through the State Department. The following day we had occasion to send a cablegram to London, and my secretary called Mr. Herter on the telephone and asked him to what person in the State Department she should send the message. She was informed that the State Department had no money to handle messages relating to the League of Nations, and that other channels would have to be used.

This information considerably perplexed me, as I could not understand why the State Department should first insist upon my sending messages through their channels, and should then decline to send them. I therefore called Mr. Herter on the telephone, and he explained that the plan to have me use the State Department channels had been definitely turned down by Mr. Lansing. He suggested that I use either the channels of the British Embassy or the War Department facilities. Later, I talked the matter over with Mr. Phillips[5] and got from him the same explanation and the same advice.

Your remarks the other day to Mr. Sweetser, therefore, in which you expressed astonishment that I am not using State Department channels, make me wonder whether I am standing on my head or my heels. Needless to say, it makes absolutely no difference to me what channels I use, provided I have some way of communicating with London. I should think that as a matter of propriety it might be more appropriate to use the State Department facilities, but as long as

---

[4] A graduate of Harvard. Special Assistant, United States Department of State. Member of Peace Commission in Paris. Member of Congress, Governor of Massachusetts, 1943-1953. Secretary of State under President Eisenhower.

[5] William Phillips was Assistant Secretary of State from January 1917 until March 1920, when he was appointed as Minister to the Netherlands and Luxemburg where he served for two years.

Secretary Lansing has ruled against it, there is no other course open to me except to use such channels as are available.

Alexander Kirk to R. B. F.

Washington   November 12, 1919

I have received your memorandum of November 11th, regarding the transmission of communications through the Department of State, and fear that Mr. Sweetser may have over-emphasized whatever remarks I may have made to him on the subject.

In reading your memorandum I find that a great many developments have occurred in this connection which I was not aware of. After your call at my office in the course of which you mentioned the possibility of receiving and sending communications through the Department of State I spoke to Mr. Herter on the matter and he, I believe, communicated with your office. The only further information which I received on the general question was merely to the effect that you had decided to send communications through the British Embassy and not through the Department of State. All the intervening developments which you enumerate in your memorandum did not come to my attention and consequently I was rather curious regarding the decision which I was told you have reached in the matter. It was this curiosity which prompted my inquiry during a general conversation with Mr. Sweetser.

I am grateful to you for explaining the situation to me and am sorry if my remarks to Mr. Sweetser bewildered you.

R. B. F. to Arthur Sweetser

Washington   November 14, 1919

Last night's meeting (of the Executive Committee of the League to Enforce Peace) [1] was one of the most exciting I

---

[1] The original and official League to Enforce Peace was started in the United States probably by Hamilton Holt, although it had its counterparts in various cities in this country and in England and

ever attended. About twenty people were present, including Taft, Lowell, Hamilton Holt, McAdoo, Vance McCormick, Hoover, Strauss, Judge Wadhams, and others. Taft and Lowell led the assault, and in the end they won their point, although it was not until they had split the organization right straight in two on partisan lines. It was really the obsequies of the League to Enforce Peace, for I think all the Democrats will now pull out. At times the meeting was positively tense, and the passages-at-arms between McAdoo and Taft were most exciting. The Republicans had the meeting packed, however, and the thing went through on a strictly party vote. What went through was a resolution to the effect that as between the defeat of the Treaty on one hand, and on the other hand acceptance of the Treaty with such reservations as could be gotten from the Senate, the League to Enforce Peace believed in the latter alternative. A second resolution followed, giving a small committee (likewise packed because McAdoo and McCormick refused to serve on it) power and authority to issue a statement whenever the moment seemed propitious. . . . .

Hitchcock sent a letter to the meeting, urging them not to take action because of the awkward situation in which it would place his attempt to obtain milder reservations, but they rode right over this letter. . . . .

In other words, the League to Enforce Peace as far as we are concerned is off the boards. They have completely reversed themselves. . . . .

R. B. F. to Sir Eric Drummond

Washington   November 14, 1919

I have prepared the enclosed memorandum as a sort of last gasp. Things are going from bad to worse, and I do not

---

Germany as well. Among its more active members were such men as ex-President Taft, President Lowell of Harvard, Theodore Marburg, and many others. At one point in its relatively brief life, both President Wilson and Senator Lodge spoke in its favor from the same platform. Senator Lodge supported the League to Enforce Peace up to the moment President Wilson endorsed it.

see any way out of the impossible situation into which the Senate has drifted. Last night I attended a long conference in New York between Mr. Taft, President Lowell, Mr. Hoover, Mr. McAdoo and one or two others, and we canvassed the situation from start to finish. I came away feeling that the thing was pretty nearly hopeless.

The enclosed memorandum will be printed and widely distributed. Of course, it is brought out anonymously because I did not feel that I could afford, as an official of the League, to get directly into this particular fight. You will appreciate, of course, that it is prepared for American consumption. I did not, therefore, take pains to correct the belief so prevalent here that America is the sole source of most of the international virtues.

I am earnestly hoping that America's failure to participate will not interfere with the plans of the League. Ultimately, in a year or two, America will be forced in by the pressure of circumstances and public opinion. With South America and Canada in and with the whole of the Eastern Hemisphere in, the United States cannot afford to stay out.

For God's sake, don't let the attitude of America disturb the thing that has been so auspiciously started. The world will never have another chance—at least not in this generation—to initiate an international project on so hopeful a basis. Of course, America's failure to participate will probably mean the withdrawal of American personnel from the Secretariat, but that is a mere incident. I am absolutely convinced that the United States will ultimately come in, only it may not be for two or three years. In the meantime, there is nothing to do but make the best possible League of Nations on the most liberal possible basis. It is commonly believed here that there cannot be a League of Nations without the United States. Personally, I admit that it will be much more difficult to constitute a League of Nations without America than with it, but I do not believe that our participation is vital.

The League can be made a going organization, and one by one the recalcitrant nations—if there are any beside the United States— will climb aboard.

These are days of great strain and stress for us over here, and of great humiliation, too. I am sure you will appreciate the position in which those of us who are working for this thing are placed.

Hamilton Fish Armstrong[1] to R. B. F.

New York   October 24, 1919

Col. House gave me this address of yours today. He seemed to think the matter was settled and that I didn't need to bother you; but it seems best for me to just send you a line and ask that when you come to New York next time you let me know when it would be convenient to see me for a moment. If you aren't going to be in New York for some time and would rather I come down to Washington of course I'll be delighted to do so.

R. B. F. to Armstrong

Washington   October 29, 1919

I have your letter of October 24th. I think the matter of your appointment is definitely settled—that is, there will be a place for you in the Section on Public Information, provided, of course, there is a League of Nations. Things look so dubious just now that all I can say is that your appointment is valid if and when the League is created. If the Senate acts favorably within a month, I do not see why you should not plan to begin your work shortly thereafter.

I do not expect to be in New York for some time. If you feel it worth while to come to Washington, I shall of course be very glad to see you.

[1] A graduate of Princeton. Member of the Editorial staff of the *New York Evening Post* from 1919 to 1921. Special correspondent in Eastern Europe from 1921 to 1922. He has been Editor of *Foreign Affairs* since 1928.

R. B. F. to Sir Eric Drummond

Washington   October 29, 1919

I cabled you the other day about the urgent need of the International Labor Conference for financial support. I have not yet had a reply, and I assume that the message may have been slightly delayed in reaching you. Briefly, the situation is this: We asked Congress for an appropriation of $200,000 to enable us to act as hosts in the proper fashion. The House bill gave us $73,000, but the Senate cut off $10,000 so that we now have a net of $63,000, thirty thousand dollars ($30,000), of which is so tied up with restrictions as to be practically useless. Butler and his crowd have made careful estimates of the cost and have prepared them on a thirty-day or a sixty-day conference. I am of the opinion that the thirty-day figure is more likely to prevail. In the cablegram that I sent you, however, I put it on a sixty-day basis, thinking that we ought to prepare for the worst in case there was a protracted session of the Labor Conference.

I am deeply humiliated over the situation, because in spite of the fact that I realize that most of this expense is a legitimate charge against the League of Nations funds, I had hoped that inasmuch as the United States government was acting as a host, we would be glad to welcome the project with warm hospitality. The feeling at the Capitol is such that this hope was bound not to be realized. The intense bitterness which exists against the President is absolutely without parallel in our history, and what the outcome is going to be I cannot see. The Senate in its determination to humiliate the President is willing to pull the world to pieces.

The Labor Conference opened this morning with a crowded house and many speeches of welcome. Varlez, in a frock coat of the vintage of the Franco-Prussian war, gladdened the eyes of all beholders. Nothing happened of any importance, but we look for some excitement either late this afternoon or tomorrow morning when the German-Austrian resolution comes up. I am sending you a copy of it herewith.

I would suggest that you use the British Foreign Office cable to communicate with me, inasmuch as I have struck a slight snag in the State Department in this connection. Sir William Tyrrell[1] has been kindness itself in putting his facilities at our disposal, and I fancy for our own communication this method is best.

R. B. F. to Huntington Gilchrist

Washington   October 29, 1919

. . . . Things are blue enough here, and in London where one is so far removed from the seat of action, they must be bluer still. But cheer up, old fellow, this thing may be pulled through yet. If it is not, we will know that we at least served in a cause that was decidedly worth while even if it failed.

The situation at the Capitol is chaotic beyond possibility of description. Just what is happening or what is going to happen no one can tell. The bitterness against the President is unspeakably intense, and in their desire to embarrass him the Republican senators are perfectly willing to pull the world to pieces. All the amendments have been defeated, but they have been rewritten in the shape of reservations and it looks as if some of them, at least, had an excellent chance of passing. Just what will happen if they are passed, no one can tell. The President is still in bed and we have no real leadership. The country is sick to death of the row and is far more interested in the industrial situation which is looming dark on the horizon. The Covenant is misunderstood and misinterpreted everywhere, and altogether, as I say, things look rather gloomy.

I am not without hope, but I do not believe it possible that the Senate can reach a decision before the first of December.

[1] He was connected with the British Foreign Office and accompanied Lord Grey to Washington when the latter was ambassador.

The Labor Conference is opening today, and we are looking forward to a merry fight on the admission of Germany and Austria. Things started off yesterday when a few South American delegates going into the Pan American building to see what the arrangements were, tore down a small Austrian flag that marked the seats where the Austrian delegates would sit if admitted. With such a spirit of brotherly love and affection, I do not know what is going to happen. . . . .

Huntington Gilchrist to R. B. F.

London   October 31, 1919

. . . . Sir Eric Drummond is rather of the impression that it would perhaps be advisable to have the seat of the League at Brussels for the next two years, say, in view of the fact that it would be much easier to get established there, and also because it is so much easier to keep in touch with Paris and London with Brussels as a center. Then, too, he feels that to give the League the support which it will need during the first few years, it is very necessary to keep in very close contact with the statesmen of the principal Allied Powers. He would not give up Geneva as the permanent seat and is of the impression that there would be less danger in moving there after a year or two when the League has been well established than there would be at present. I think it is quite possible that this matter may come up at the second Council meeting. . . . .

R. B. F. to Huntington Gilchrist

Washington   November 14, 1919

. . . . Suppose I take up the points that you mention one by one.

SEAT OF THE LEAGUE

I have no particular objection to Brussels (as the seat of the League), but I know that the President and Colonel House have very pronounced objections, particularly the

President. He feels that the anti-German feeling will be so strong in Belgium that for many years the environment there will be an unhappy one, and that an organization striving to be absolutely neutral might under the circumstances have a difficult time. For that reason he not only pushed but insisted upon Geneva. Colonel House echoes the President's feeling in this respect. Of course, at the time Geneva was chosen, it was not foreseen that there would be the delay that has ensued, and it is possible that the President might consent to a temporary shift of arrangements. However, I have not been able to see him because of his illness, and Colonel House has been out of town. I know, however, that Colonel House would be very dubious about it until he had a talk with the President.

There is something in Drummond's argument that for a year or two it might be advisable to keep nearer the heart of things than would be possible if we were located in Geneva; but would it not mean that if we were temporarily located in Brussels, we would never move to Geneva? That is, it would then be increasingly difficult to break away. I should hesitate to have the League take a step now that would saddle us with an undesirable site, and that is my only reason for feeling that we ought not to give up Geneva unless the arguments on the other side are absolutely insuperable. I admit that this is a rather non-commital answer, but it is the best I can do under the circumstances without being able to talk with the people here. I do not see any reason, however, why the matter should not appear on the agenda of the Council for full consideration.

LABOR CONFERENCE

I suppose by the time this letter reaches you, you will know that the matter of transporting the German delegates has been settled one way or another. We have been up against an impossible proposition. Secretary Baker, upon my personal solicitation, finally gave orders that the transports were to be used to bring over the Labor delegates.

Then twenty-four hours later he made an exception of the Germans and Austrians because he felt that with thousands of American troops on the boat, he could not guarantee the safety of the delegates of the Central Powers, and he was fearful that some act of indignity or even worse might occur which would upset things for months to come. In this position I think he was probably well advised.

We then made every effort to find out from commercial steamship lines what could be done, but we met with no success. Frankly, the English and French lines did not care to bring over the German delegates, and were disinclined to make any arrangements to that end. I presume they felt that it would hurt their trade. We took it up with some of the neutral lines—that is, the Red Star and one or two others, and were told that the arrangement would have to be made on the other side. That is why I cabled you as I did. Incidentally, as you know, the Labor Conference went on record in expressing its urgent hope that the German delegates would get here, and I feel we did everything from this end that could possibly be done. It was an unfortunate circumstance, but I do not see how it could be avoided—certainly as far as Washington was concerned.

CABLES

The Military Intelligence people here tell me that Lieber's code is a non-workable proposition because it is a commercial code and its vocabulary is very limited and inadequate. I do not believe that it will be necessary to transmit messages in code as long as we have the British wires at our disposal. If, however, you want to get in touch with me in absolute confidence, I would suggest that you use Lieber's code with the arrangement suggested in your letter of October 31st, and I have therefore cabled you today, "Code alteration approved." It may not be necessary to use this channel of communication, but if it is necessary, we will consider this arrangement satisfactory.

I have been having a devil of a time with the State Department about our cablegrams, and hereafter I think I shall reach you either through the British wires or by commercial wires. The State Department is scared pink for fear that the Senate will find out that I am having some privileges over here. For sheer pusillanimity, commend me to some of the officials of the State Department. . . . .

SITUATION IN THE SENATE

The situation in the Senate is desperate, and we cannot tell today which of the following courses will be followed:

a) A filibuster by Reed, Borah, etc., which will throw the thing over into the next Congress—a course of action which really means defeat.

b) Deadlock between the Republicans and Democrats over the fourteen reservations now pending before the Senate, the Republicans being unable to get the two-thirds vote needed for ratification, and the Democrats being unable to defeat the reservations.

c) Absolute defeat of the Treaty by the Democrats because of the drastic character of the reservations.

d) Some compromise between the Republicans and the Democrats over the reservations as they now stand.

Of course, the last step is the one we will wish for, but I am not at all certain that it can be brought about. I have never seen such bitterness as exists at the present time in the Senate and elsewhere. Publicity as regards the danger of delay, etc., is of absolutely no avail because the Senate doesn't care two hangs about public opinion. It has completely isolated itself from any external influence, and as a matter of fact I am not sure but that there may not be a substantial body of citizens in America who would gladly see the Treaty defeated and the League thrown out. The volume of misrepresentation about the League has been so enormous that everybody is confused and alarmed, and the Senate in its play of protecting American interests, has, I am afraid, a very substantial body of support behind it. . . . .

R. B. F. to Sir Eric Drummond

November 20, 1919

I sent you today the following cable:

"Action of Senate last night was decisive and I do not see any possibility of a change in position. Even if the Democrats had consented to the reservations which the Republicans attached to the Treaty, I cannot believe that these reservations would have been acceptable to the Allied Powers. The Senate has adjourned and will not meet until December first. The President will probably re-submit the Treaty at that time, but as the personnel of the Senate will be the same as at present, there is no prospect of favorable action. Personally, I believe that the matter will become an issue in the Presidential campaign in November, 1920, and that the adherence of the United States before that date cannot be looked for. This brings up the whole question of the continuance of American personnel on the Secretariat of the League. I shall see Colonel House about the matter tonight and will get an interview with the President next week if his condition permits. I would appreciate it if you would cable fully and frankly your views."

Needless to say, we are plunged in gloom. Until the last moment I hoped for some compromise, but the situation grew more and more rigid as time went on, and the Treaty was finally defeated in a condition of deadlock. The reservations which the Republicans proposed were sweeping and drastic, and as I told you in my cablegram, I do not believe that they would have been accepted by the Allied Powers. Certainly if any one of the Allied Powers had attempted to attach similar reservations to its adherence, the United States would have been the first to object. To me—and I believe to thousands of Americans around the country—it is a matter of great national humiliation. We have sowed the wind, and who knows what the reaping will be.

League of Nations

I am in great doubt about the question of the continuance of the American personnel on the Secretariat. I think it should be looked at from two angles: first, whether the other nations would care to have any Americans on the Secretariat, and second, whether representation on the Secretariat would prejudice our efforts here to put America into the League of Nations. The first point is, of course, the more important one, for I feel that America has forfeited almost any claim to have her point of view considered in this matter. My first reaction—and I confess that it is not a considered one—is that it would be unwise for any Americans to be attached to the Secretariat. As far as I am concerned, my resignation is in your hands, and you are free to accept it at any time. I should like, however, to talk the matter over with Colonel House, and perhaps with the President if I can see him, and I hope too that you will give me your frank opinion on the situation. The fate of the world is bound up in this question of a League, and personal considerations, of course, have no place.

I am assuming in all this that there will be a League of Nations, and I sincerely hope that your plan in this respect will not miscarry. I believe that immediately there will be organized in America a great movement to put us in. I should hope that it could be formed on a non-political basis so that both parties would see the handwriting on the wall and would realize that no jugglery or jockeying is going to defeat the determined purpose of the great mass of the American people. It may take two or three years to accomplish it, but I am confident that it will ultimately go through. We have in this country now two organizations: one, the League to Enforce Peace, and the other, the League of Free Nations. Neither organization, I believe, can effectively lead in this new movement. I should hope for a new non-partisan, non-political League of Nations Union, whose sole aim would be to put America in. This presupposes, of course, a *going* League that embraces not only the countries in the eastern

71

hemisphere, but those of the western hemisphere as well. Our hopes and best wishes will therefore follow you in your effort to get the League on its feet. We are humiliated that we cannot join in the project, but the American people, I believe, are committed to a League of Nations, and the question will never be settled until she is a member. I trust you will write me with the utmost frankness about this whole business.

R. B. F. to Colonel House

Washington   November 25, 1919

In accordance with our arrangement, I saw (Attorney General) Gregory this morning and after a short talk with him we adjourned to Baker's office where we discussed the matter for some time. Baker concurred absolutely in your opinion that the President ought not to send any message to the Senate about the Treaty, or make any reference to it in any way. So far we four all were agreed. Baker felt, however, that it would be better for the President not to take any step of any kind for two or three weeks after the Senate convened. He thought that strong forces were moving in America in the direction of forcing the Republicans to come to terms, and that if the President showed a disposition to keep the Treaty pigeonholed, it would not be long before the Republicans would be put in the position of asking for it privately. However, Baker felt that the difference between your program and his program was slight, and that the important thing was to keep the President from making any statement to the Senate. He therefore concurred heartily in your letters, and Gregory made an engagement to present them to Mrs. Wilson sometime today. I have not seen Gregory since, but I am to take dinner with him tonight and I shall let you know the result immediately.

R. B. F. to Huntington Gilchrist

Washington   November 25, 1919

I have your confidential letter of October 25th in regard to the possibility of General Harbord's[1] appointment at Dantzig and Mr. Taft's appointment on the Council. I agree with both these propositions—at least I agree with the first very heartily, and with the second to a qualified degree. I have talked over with Secretary Baker the possibility of getting General Harbord, and Baker is most cordial in his reception of the idea. We might have some difficulty in landing the General, but he would certainly be a wonder.

I should like to see somebody like Mr. Taft appointed on the Council, but Taft has wobbled so in the last two or three weeks that I am in despair about him. However, your general proposition is good, and we may be able to do something with it.

You will appreciate, of course, that with the situation as it is here just now, nothing at all can be done along these lines. We are in the depths of despair. Whether a compromise is going to be possible when the Senate reconvenes, nobody knows, but personally I am rather doubtful. I am afraid that the only avenue open for a compromise is to have the President do all the compromising and give up the whole game. However, by the time this reaches you, something will probably have developed. I spend all my time between here and New York as a sort of liaison between Colonel House and the White House.

Don't get unduly discouraged. However this thing comes out, whether we win or lose, we will always be glad to have participated in so worth while an attempt.

R. B. F. to Sir Eric Drummond

Washington   November 25, 1919

The Labor Conference will adjourn this coming Saturday

[1] Chief of Staff to General Pershing in France and later placed in charge of the Army's Service of Supply (S.O.S.).

November twenty-ninth, and most of the delegates are slated for immediate return. I am sorry to have to report that they are going home in a spirit of bitterness and disillusion-ment—glad to get away from Washington, and vowing, many of them, never to return. This feeling is so widespread among the delegates and its repercussions will so soon be felt in Europe, that I think I ought to describe, somewhat at length perhaps, the various factors which have led up to it.

1. The Labor delegates undoubtedly thought that they were coming to a country where the idea of international cooperation, as embodied in a League of Nations, was warmly and enthusiastically sponsored. President Wilson's work in Europe, and the emphasis which had been placed upon the new order in international relations, gave them the right to believe that inasmuch as they represented the first tangible beginning of the new machinery, they and their work would be received in America with generous hospital-ity. Instead, they found a country that was confused and torn with doubts about the whole conception of a League of Nations. Their work was conducted in Washington, which was the storm center of the debate. They saw the League kicked about the political arena with the apparent approval of many powerful interests and newspapers, and finally defeated in a debate that was wholly partisan in character, the result of which was applauded in many parts of the country.

They were not in a position to see or to understand the silent forces in America, represented in thousands of homes and communities, that are looking and working for the League. All that the delegates could know is that loud and vociferous interests shrieked hysterically against American cooperation in any international movement and apparently won the fight. Consequently, these delegates are going home convinced either that America's early belief in a League of Nations was hypocritical and insincere, or that President Wilson's work in Europe was a false pretense. They are utterly disillusioned about America, and they believe that light and leading cannot be looked for here. I am sure that among the European delegates there would scarcely be a single vote that would favor another international meeting of any kind in Washington.

2. Another factor in this feeling of bitterness is the environment of industrial conflict in which the meetings of the Conference were held. By an unhappy coincidence, the meetings were staged in the midst of the two greatest strikes in America's history—the steel strike and the coal strike. The drastic methods to which the Government resorted to break these strikes have made a most unfavorable impression upon the Conference. The novel use of the injunction as a weapon of industrial warfare, the employment of the State constabulary in Pennsylvania to break up meetings of strikers, and the generally hostile attitude of the press toward the attempts of the Unions to obtain recognition, have given the delegates from Europe the impression that America is the center of industrial Bourbonism.

Moreover, the delegates have seen the great confusion of thought that exists in America in regard to industrial unrest, by which liberalism in any form is made synonymous with radicalism, and labor unionists, mild socialists or any persons who dare to think along unusual lines, are indiscriminately dubbed "anarchists," "reds" and "Bolsheviks." They have seen a great popular wave of "heresy hunting" sweep over the country, accompanied by raids and lynchings. They have been holding their meetings in an environment that was distinctly hostile to the very program which they were invited here to discuss.

3. The hostility and indifference of America to the Labor Conference has been distinctly shown in the press. *The Washington Post,* which is perhaps our most important local paper here at the Capitol, has followed the conference in attack after attack, calling the representatives "waifs," "strays," "reds," etc. Two or three New York and Chicago papers have been almost equally bitter. *The Washington Post* is far too extreme to be typical of the attitude of the

American press as a whole, but it is the paper which is most widely read by the delegates. Moreover, the delegates are convinced, I believe, that there has been a conspiracy of silence among those papers which did not positively attack them. Many prominent papers have scarcely mentioned the Conference. Personally, I do not believe that this belief has any foundation. The news of the Labor Conference has been literally crowded out of the papers by the industrial situation and the Treaty debate. It is true, however, that quite apart from any feeling of hostility, the American newspapers have not treated the Conference with any degree of seriousness, and that little interest has been displayed by the reading public.

4. The Conference has been attacked not only by the press, but by public officials. The speech of Senator Sherman, of Illinois, in protesting against the influx from Europe of the "dangerous radicals and anarchists" assembled at Washington, was bitterly resented by the Conference. This speech was followed by others of like tenor, and just before it adjourned, the Senate passed a reservation to the Treaty excluding the United States from participation in the Labor Conference except upon such terms as Congress itself might name. Inasmuch as the Conference was meeting at Washington under the urgent invitation of the President and with the approval of Congress, this last step was regarded as a crowning insult.

5. Another factor in the bitterness with which the Conference is adjourning, is the utter lack of courtesy on the part of the United States Government in welcoming and entertaining the delegates. It is now well known among the delegates that Congress refused to supply the necessary funds and that money had to be obtained from Europe. The illness of the President made it impossible for him to take any action along the line of official entertainment, and the State Department, because of its fear of the Senate, refused to participate. Consequently, there was scarcely any official recognition of the Conference. Some two weeks after the

Conference opened, the Vice President came to the hall one afternoon and shook hands with the delegates, and later the Navy Department arranged a trip down the Potomac to Washington's tomb. But apart from these two incidents, there has been no official act of hospitality. Invitations to a reception to the Conference, extended by a Republican Senator, were subsequently withdrawn—an act which increased the strain of an already strained situation. The Conference has been snubbed officially and socially, and I doubt if any international gathering was ever held under more unhappy auspices.

I have written at length because I know that you will hear much of this in Europe. I confess, too, that I have written with a deep sense of humiliation. Under the circumstances I am forced to the opinion that the League should take careful thought before scheduling another international meeting of any kind in Washington.

R. B. F. to Sir Eric Drummond

November 26, 1919

I sent you today the following cable:

"*Confidential.* With further reference to my cable number 1595 there is some slight hope that basis for compromise will be found when Senate convenes on December first, but I am not optimistic. The Republicans are rigid in their determination to reject any suggested changes in the reservations, with the possible exception of the preamble, which has to do with the method by which the Powers are to signify their acceptance of the reservations. The President's illness makes it impossible for anyone to talk with him on this matter. Senator Hitchcock, the leader of the Democratic party in the Senate, has seen him twice, but I understand the conversation has been only of a general nature. Colonel House is not allowed to see him and I am afraid that he does not read the letters that are sent him. I see no prospect of a solution of this question before

January. I assume that the Powers will go ahead with the League without the United States."

It may be idle to write you about this matter, because it is likely that there will be great changes in the situation before the letter reaches you. I am afraid that America has gotten herself into a cul-de-sac from which an exit cannot readily be found. If the President were not so ill, I believe that some basis of agreement could be discovered; but as I told you in my cablegram, nobody sees him, not even Colonel House, and he is completely shut off from the rest of the world. Senator Hitchcock has had two general conversations with him, and Secretary Baker has seen him once. Baker tells me that the President's mind is clear and concise, but that he is physically very, very weak.

A huge propaganda is starting in the country to force some kind of a compromise, and I enclose herewith a copy of a full-page advertisement which will appear in every newspaper in the two hundred largest cities and towns of the United States. The difficulty is that there is perhaps an equally forceful propaganda—and certainly a more appealing propaganda—on the other side, urging the Senators to stand by their reservations, on the ground that these reservations have protected American interests which were overlooked in Paris. This, of course, is a popular jingo argument which appeals to the unthinking, and it is difficult to meet it. Every newspaper is now featuring the reservations, and they are the center of popular discussion everywhere. I cannot help thinking that the feeling is growing in America that they ought to be sustained. That is, the President's position of no reservations, or at most, mild reservations, is fast losing ground and we are reaching a point where popular opinion will back up a demand for *all* the reservations or no Treaty. The Republicans touched a sensitive chord when they launched their movement on the grounds of "Americanizing" the Covenant.

If, therefore, in order to save the Treaty here, the President should bow to the Republicans and accept their fourteen reservations, the Powers would find themselves in an extremely awkward position in determining whether or not they should concede the terms upon which America conditions her ratification. They would find themselves, I am afraid, arrayed against a public opinion in the United States determined not to yield, and it is possible that the refusal of the Powers to accept some of the reservations, instead of being a boomerang for the Senate, as the President's party evidently hopes, would be turned into a wave of jingo feeling against the Powers themselves.

Of course, any speculation about this thing is, after all, only speculation and there may be other views that are more optimistic or better based than mine. I have never seen such a pitch of political bitterness as we have here now, nor did I ever realize that America could be so completely misinformed as she is about the essential *facts* of a great political dispute. . . . .

R. B. F. to Sir Eric Drummond

Washington   November 27, 1919

I cabled you today as follows:

"Your cables number 2103 and 2112 and Gilchrist's cable number 2104 in regard to Americans on the Secretariat. I have talked the matter over with Colonel House and others. We believe that within the next three or four weeks we shall know pretty definitely what the Senate is going to do. We therefore are inclined to concur in your suggestion that for the time being Americans retain their membership on the Secretariat. If during this period it is necessary for you to obtain the confirmation of the Council for the appointments already made, United States citizens will be placed on a temporary and provisional list. If, at the end of three or four weeks, it appears that the Senate will not ratify the Treaty or that its ratification will be unduly delayed, it is my personal belief that those

Americans whose work is semi-political in character should immediately resign. This includes Beer, Sweetser, Gilchrist and myself and perhaps Hudson. Whether the Americans whose work is entirely technical in character, like Miss Wilson, Pierce, etc., should resign, is a matter for you to determine. In any event, I am anxious that you should not be embarrassed in any way by the presence at this time of an American Under Secretary General on the Secretariat. If, therefore, in the next three or four weeks my relationship to the Secretariat should prove awkward, please consider that my resignation is in your hands for immediate action."

I talked over this matter at dinner the other night with Lord Grey, Sir William Tyrrell, Colonel House, and others, and they were all of the opinion that my resignation at this time, or the resignation of any of the Americans on the Secretariat, would be considered by the Senate as a confession of defeat. For that reason, it seemed wise to stay on until we could be certain just what action the Senate intended to take.

In the event that the Senate ratified, the position of the Americans, as you say, will be quite regular. There are two other courses, however, which the Senate can take. It can definitely refuse to ratify, or it can postpone consideration, leaving the whole thing in the air. If it refuses absolutely to ratify, and the matter is thrown over until the Presidential campaign, I should think that resignations on the part of the Americans would be immediately in order. If it postpones consideration, it is probable that it would call for the same action on our part, although the matter could be considered in the light of the new situation.

I appreciate very much the sentence in your cablegram in regard to your personal hope to retain the services of the Americans, despite the action of the Senate. There would, of course, be nothing in law or ethics that would prevent citizens of the United States from serving on the Secretariat, even if America were not herself a member of the League; but it does not seem to me possible that the Council would consent to this arrangement, and I am not sure that it would be at all wise. While of course in theory, members of the Secretariat are chosen on the basis of ability alone, in practice nationality plays a very important part, as you know, and I do not believe that the representatives of non-member States could be nearly so useful or effective as the representatives of member nations. It seems to me that in the event America does not join the League, the only thing that would justify the Secretary General in retaining the services of an American would be that no other person of the same caliber and degree of efficiency could be found in any of the member States. This contingency is, of course, out of the question, and on the basis of this theory it would not be necessary for any American to retain his post.

As you surely know, I am more anxious to serve the League of Nations than do anything else in the world, and even if I sever my connection with the Secretariat, I am not going to desert the cause. It is entirely possible, however, that my continued connection with the Secretariat may do more harm than good, and it is for that reason that I am anxious that you should use your own judgment as to when my resignation should be accepted. Just as soon as the situation develops here to a point where I believe that my continued association is detrimental, I shall instantly resign; but I am particularly anxious that during this period you too should use your judgment about the situation on the other side, and should feel free at any time to accept my resignation as if it were already in your hands.

What a tragedy this whole business is, and how different from the fond dreams which we had this summer.

R. B. F. to Sir Eric Drummond

Washington   December 1, 1919

I have talked over with Colonel House the compromise proposed in your letter of October 4th to make Brussels the headquarters of the League for the time being. Monnet's point, as I understand it, is that Geneva should be announced by the Council as the permanent seat, and that instructions should be given to proceed with the purchase of the site and the erection of buildings. However, until the buildings were ready, headquarters should be provided in Brussels. For the first two years this would give us the opportunity to keep in close contact with the western Powers.

I find Colonel House unalterably opposed to this scheme and he is confident that in this matter he is speaking the President's opinion. He believes that even the temporary choice of Brussels would give strong emphasis to the belief widely held in many quarters, that the League of Nations is, after all, only an alliance of victorious Powers. He is firmly convinced of the necessity of having the seat of the League immediately located in a neutral country, and he is fearful that any change in this program would involve us in unfortunate consequences.

I can only give you the colonel's opinion. I may add, however, that he was most emphatic about it.

As I write today, it looks as if the deadlock in the Senate is not going to be broken, so that this question may perhaps be one upon which the opinion of the United States will be superfluous. Of course, we are assuming that whether the United States joins or not, a League of Nations will be brought into being. . . . .

Sir Eric Drummond to R. B. F.

London   December 15, 1919

Many thanks for your letter of November 27 with regard to the general position in America, and particularly that of the American members of the International Secretariat.

So long as there is any prospect of the Senate's coming to a definite decision one way or the other within a reasonable time, the position of Americans on the Secretariat should, I am quite clear, remain as at present—at any rate unless this would unfavourably affect the chances of the League in the Senate. I will not in this letter go into what ought to be done if the Senate refuses to ratify, or postpones its consideration indefinitely. We should probably be guided by developments in America and by the general feeling in the Council. At any rate, you need not be afraid of the slightest difficulty in connection with your presence on the Secretariat, as far as opinion outside America is concerned. As regards opinion inside, I feel that you are much better able to judge.

Lord Robert Cecil saw Clemenceau when he was over, and urged on him very strongly, as his personal view, that the French and British Governments ought to be prepared to accept all the Republican reservations, provided that the preamble were eliminated. He also informed Lord Curzon of his opinion. I do not know whether what he said was taken up, but he was, I feel sure, right.

The economic position of the world has become such that disaster in Europe of a most appalling kind is imminent unless American cooperation can be secured without delay; and if such cooperation is to be secured by American ratification of the Treaty and Covenant, it is worth paying almost any price to obtain ratification. Unless international action is taken, all the most prominent economists predict such economic conditions in practically every European country as must lead to what will be equivalent to revolution and the break-up of civilisation in its present form. America herself would not come out of such a crisis unscathed, unless she could do without exports to Europe by consuming and making use of all she produces herself. Even if she achieved this end, the period of transition must lead to great distress and disturbance. It may, of course, be that America will cooperate without having ratified the Treaty and being outside the League. If she does so, I shall be glad, because I do not want to see European disaster; but I doubt whether in those circumstances the League would ever be an international instrument of really first-class importance. It would become a centre for those subjects of international life where no conflict is likely to arise.

What I therefore hope to see is America cooperating as a member of the League. I doubt whether many people here realise the facts as to the world financial and economic position. If they did, they would regard it as the only matter of importance, and all these territorial difficulties could probably be easily adjusted.

P.S. If the reservations were accepted as they stand, with the exception of the preamble, we should, I hope, secure the complete cooperation of the Republicans in making the League a success. We should then have united America behind us.

Huntington Gilchrist to R. B. F. (cablegram)

London December 2, 1919

Would it not be wise to suggest liaison State Department and League after deposit of ratification and during the time of uncertainty in the immediate future? For following reasons this should be done; first, for the protection of American interests; second, for obtaining information as to League action; third, for preventing any action in the internal organization of the League which would be prejudicial to eventual American participation. . . . .

R. B. F. to Huntington Gilchrist

Washington December 8, 1919

I cabled you today as follows:

"Your cable in regard to liaison with State Department received. I agree in your statement, but unfortunately it is impossible at this moment for me to suggest it. State Department is not in condition to receive such a suggestion just now. Am writing."

The situation is just this: My sole hold on this proposition over here is through the President. The President is ill, and I have not been able to see him. I have no standing with the State Department whatever and I do not believe that any representative of the League of Nations just now, even if he were the angel Gabriel himself, would have any standing. Between you and me, I do not believe that Lansing has any particular sympathy with the League, and certainly the attitude of the men around him during my stay here has been one of veiled hostility. In large part I think it is due to their fear of the Senate. So that while your suggestion is excellent, I am not in a position to take any step on it. The State Department is inherently sore because State Department personnel were not appointed to the League. At least, this is my personal belief. . . . .

R. B. F. to Sir Eric Drummond

Washington   December 19, 1919

I wish I could send you as a Christmas greeting the news that the United States had decided to ratify the Treaty without reservations. Unfortunately, however, I am unable to do it. The matter seemed to be proceeding the other day toward a possible compromise, when the President issued his no-compromise statement, which upset the whole apple cart. So that now things are just milling around in the Senate, with no tangible head or tail to the situation. I am afraid the President is badly misinformed about the development of public opinion here at home. You see, he is completely shut off from the rest of the world by reason of his illness, and he sees scarcely anybody. Colonel House has not talked with him since he returned, and Lansing and others who might be in a position to inform him of the trend of events have not seen him for months. I doubt if Polk can see him when he returns. The President is losing ground rapidly with public opinion, particularly since his no-compromise statement of last Sunday. Even the *New York World* and the *New York Globe*, which have backed him up to the limit through thick and thin, have been lukewarm in the last few days. The country is disgusted with the failure of its authorities to put through some kind of a treaty. . . . .

R. B. F. to William Howard Taft

Washington   December 22, 1919

For some five or six months I have been serving as Under Secretary General of the provisional organization of the League of Nations in London, working in conjunction with Sir Eric Drummond. I came over to Washington to represent Sir Eric at the International Labor Conference, and have postponed my return, pending action by the Senate. I am venturing to write you because for some time I have felt that the Senate's reservation relating to domestic questions (number five) is going to prove a serious stumbling block with the Allies. A private letter from Drummond today confirms this belief. Drummond feels that most of the reservations proposed by the Senate are innocuous as far as the League is concerned—that is, they relate to questions of local policy in which the League has no interest, or they raise problems which will prove largely academic. His chief anxiety is in regard to the reservation about disarmament (in which he concurs with the judgment expressed in your analysis in the *Philadelphia Ledger*) and to the reservation about domestic matters, which I have just mentioned. It is in relation to this latter reservation that I am addressing you. You will understand, of course, that I am writing on my own initiative, and in a purely private capacity.

In an analysis of the reservations which I prepared for the State Department a number of weeks ago, I made the following comment on this reservation:

"This reservation vitiates the whole covenant. It is so drawn as to be all-inclusive. If a nation reserves to itself exclusively the right to decide what questions are within its domestic jurisdiction, it is free to name practically any question which its selfish interest may dictate. The clause is nearly as vague as the phrase 'national honor' and 'vital interests' which have been universally recognized as barriers to all real international cooperation.

"Suppose this reservation became general. Italy might perfectly well fly in the face of world opinion by calling the Adriatic problem a 'domestic' issue. Japan could easily stretch the phrase to cover her Asiatic Monroe Doctrine. The states which have been made to agree to respect minorities within their borders, Poland, Czecho-Slovakia, Roumania, and Greece might endeavor to recoil under this phrase from what is recognized as one of the real advances made by the Peace Conference. In short, the clause is so inclusive as to open the door to all sorts of selfish policies and prevent the operation of a general world judgment on affairs properly of world concern.

"Take also the word 'commerce.' The United States would consider its 'commerce' wholly within its own jurisdiction. But part of this 'commerce' is international. Part of it goes into foreign parts at the courtesy of the foreign governments. It is dependent on foreign laws and foreign regulations. Can we maintain that American 'commerce' is purely a domestic issue? Moreover, there is an obvious confusion of thought as to the attempt to suppress the traffic in women and children, and in opium and other dangerous drugs. The Covenant seeks to remedy these evils, not in their domestic aspect within the boundaries of a single state, but in their international aspect as between states, especially as between member states and backward countries. This phase of the evil can be reached only by international agreement, and the clause in the Covenant providing for systematic suppression has generally been regarded as one of the great humanitarian advances made by the Treaty. Yet this reservation prevents these questions, so far as the United States is concerned, from being considered by any agency of the League, despite the fact that the United States has hitherto led the world in this field.

"The inclusion of the word 'labor' in the reservation debars American participation in the International Labor Conference or the International Labor Office, for no question relating to American labor may be submitted to the consideration of any agency of the League. The United States, therefore, could not sit in any conference discussing world labor problems if in the course of that discussion American labor conditions were in any way considered. Hence, one could not discuss for instance the international limitation of immigration if it were necessary to discuss whether the American labor supply were sufficient, nor could American progress in labor advancement be used as an example to bring more backward states up to its own level. Whatever may be gained by common international action in bettering labor standards is lost through this reservation." . . . .

While I am convinced that reservations are absolutely essential, and that a spirit of compromise is necessary all around if we are going to get the treaty through, I concur with you in deprecating the necessity for attaching any reservations. . . . .

In this connection, Drummond makes the following comment in a letter which I recently had from him:

"I cannot foretell what the attitude of the British Government will be towards the League if America fails to ratify, or ratifies with stiff reservations. Bonar Law promised recently in the House of Commons that the British Government would give the League full support whatever happened, but at the same time there is a strong feeling in Government circles here in favour of drastic revision of the Covenant. This feeling derives extra force from possible American reservations. It is not suggested that such a revision should take place immediately, but it may be demanded after, say, a year's experience of the working of the Covenant. American reservations would be used as the lever to persuade public opinion of the necessity for such revision. Personally, I do not think that a revision in itself must necessarily be bad, but from the quarters from which the proposal emanates, I suspect that it may be inspired from a desire to weaken international cooperation and to exalt nationalism."

You will understand, I am sure, the frankness and confidence with which I am writing. I had the pleasure of meeting you for a moment at a dinner given at the League of Nations office a month ago, but the discussion which followed was so hectic that I did not have an opportunity to talk with you. If I can be of any service, please do not hesitate to command me.

William Howard Taft to R. B. F.

New Haven   December 24, 1919

I have your letter of December 22nd and thank you for writing it and for giving me the inside from the foreign standpoint. The truth is, we might as well recognize that the attitude of the Senate is such that the other countries are bound to treat the United States as a spoiled child, and count on her doing her part in spite of her reservations. Of course domestic questions are not domestic questions, if they are incorporated in a treaty. I don't think that even such men as Lodge and Knox would contend that. If they are made the subject of a treaty, they are given an international aspect, and of course are subject to the consideration of the League Tribunals. I doubt if it would be wise to raise the question, but I shall read over carefully what you say and write you again.

R. B. F. and Arthur Sweetser to Sir Eric Drummond

Washington   December 25, 1919

The American Members of the Secretariat in the United States[1] cannot allow the Christmas season to pass without

[1] The group comprised Arthur Sweetser, Manley Hudson, George Beer, and R. B. F.

sending a message of friendship and good wishes to their colleagues overseas. Though the present period may indeed seem a dark one for the ideals we all cherish, nevertheless we over here hope and believe that light will soon break. Meanwhile the present world disorganization and suffering offer to those who believe in international cooperation and goodwill a challenge for redoubled efforts. May next Christmas see us all together at Geneva helping to build towards that better future which the suffering of the War justify the world in expecting.

R. B. F. to Sir Eric Drummond

Washington   December 30, 1919

There is still little to report, although it is now pretty evident that Senator Knox's resolution ratifying the treaty without the League will fail. Moreover, there is a growing feeling that some form of reservations will be found which can command the support of sixty-four senators. To do this is going to require a lot of jockeying and compromising, in which the rival ambitions, not only of the two parties, but of the several factions within each party, will be sadly mixed up. I think, therefore, that if it is accomplished it is going to take a longer time than is now generally admitted by our more hopeful optimists. As far as I can see now, the only possible basis of compromise which can get a two-third's vote will be the Lodge reservations slightly modified. These modifications are apt to be in the preamble (eliminating the necessity of other powers formally agreeing to the reservations) ; in the reservation on Article X; in the reservation on Shantung (making it a bit more palatable) and perhaps in the reservation on the vote of the British Dominions (eliminating the offensive second part) . I cannot see at the present time any hope of changing the reservation in regard to domestic questions, or the reservation in regard to disarmament. So that what we are apt to get out of a compromise will not be much of an improvement over the original recommendations of the Foreign Affairs Committee.

Assuming, however, that we get this much, a more serious hurdle, as I wrote you before, is presented by the attitude of the President. Nobody knows and nobody can find out what he is going to do. The most intimate reports that I can get are to the effect that he is in a bitter mood and disinclined to yield on any point. As I wrote Gilchrist the other day, I cannot help thinking that he may prefer to go down to defeat, if necessary, in the belief that history will ultimately vindicate his position, and mark him as a prophet who lived before his time. His complete isolation from everybody who can influence him, makes it impossible to bring any pressure to bear, and while we may be wrong in our surmises, I am exceedingly fearful that the President may adopt a rigid and uncompromising course. What a pity that the forces on both sides in this controversy should be carried away by verbal interpretations, sacrificing the spirit for the letter!

I am in close touch with the leaders on both sides, although my efforts, I am afraid, are futile enough. I have recently been trying to convert Mr. Taft as to his position on the reservation regarding domestic questions. Taft frankly does not like the reservation, but he doesn't feel that it is particularly dangerous. His whole position is that America will play the game anyway, regardless of the reservations that she writes down at the beginning. By the way, did you happen to notice the estimate of Senator Spencer, of Missouri, on the staggering cost of the Secretariat of the League of Nations? He believes that it will require 185,000 employees, whose salary roll will mount to $460,000,000 a year. He further makes the modest estimate for "printing, exclusive of labor, plants, furniture, office equipment, attendance, witnesses at hearings, etc." at $500,000,000 per annum. Unavoidable extras swell the total of the Secretariat's annual expense account to $1,194,592,090. His final argument is that inasmuch as the United States is the richest country in the world just at present, we will have to pay most of this.

If this estimate is accurate, poor Ames[1] is going to have his hands full handling his job, and I think he ought to begin to look around for assistance right away. Whatever our senators lack—and I concede that they are lacking in many things—as a loyal American I protest that they are not lacking in imagination!

R. B. F. to William Howard Taft

Washington   January 5, 1920

. . . . I have just had a letter from Sir Eric Drummond in which he paints a rather gloomy picture of the situation in Europe. He says:

"The economic position of the world has become such that disaster in Europe of a most appalling kind is imminent, unless American cooperation can be secured without delay; and if such cooperation is to be secured by American ratification of the Treaty and Covenant, it is worth paying almost any price to obtain ratification. Unless international action is taken, all the most prominent economists predict such economic conditions in practically every European country as must lead to what will be equivalent to revolution and the break-up of civilization in its present form. America herself would not come out of such a crisis unscathed, unless she could do without exports to Europe by consuming and making use of all she produces herself. Even if she achieved this end, the period of transition must lead to great distress and disturbance. It may, of course, be that America will cooperate without having ratified the Treaty and being outside the League. If she does so, I shall be glad, because I do not want to see European disaster; but I doubt whether in those circumstances the League would ever be an international instrument of really first-class importance. It would become a centre for those subjects of international life where no conflict is likely to arise."   . . . .

[1] Financial director of the League of Nations from 1919 to 1926.

William Howard Taft to R. B. F.

New Haven   January 6, 1920

I have your letter of January 5th. Drummond's attitude seems to be that they are likely to accept whatever we put in the form of ratification, and I hope they will. I don't think the reservations are going to make a great deal of difference.

But that is no reason why we should not make the reservations as soft as we can. [This sentence in Mr. Taft's own handwriting.]

R. B. F. to Sir Eric Drummond

Washington   January 5, 1920

Many thanks for your letter of December 15th in regard to the situation in Europe. Your description of the economic condition and of the imminence of disaster, is, I confess, most appalling. While our papers on the Atlantic seaboard carry something of this news, in the interior and in the west there is no knowledge of it whatever, and the country as a whole is so fed up with the row over its foreign relations that it is difficult for any group to start any effective propaganda. Taft and a few others are doing heroic work, but it is against a current that is running strongly in the opposite direction.

There is no particular news from Washington. The Senate convenes today, and while there is some optimistic talk about the possibility of immediate agreement on reservations, I confess I do not see at present any particular basis for it. The two camps seem to be as far apart as ever, and the attitude of the President is still an unknown quantity. The total rejectionists are manoeuvering very cleverly to throw the thing into the campaign next fall, although I am confident that the majority of the Senate—certainly of the country—is anxious to have the matter cleared up and out of the way.

The postscript to your letter is a bit disquieting: "If the reservations were accepted as they stand, with the exception of the preamble, we should, I hope, secure the complete co-operation of the Republicans in making the League a success. We should then have united America behind us." I sincerely hope that this statement of the case is correct. One cannot help noticing, however, the temptation which the situation presents to the Republicans to glorify the part which they are playing in preventing the acceptance of the treaty without reservations. Their claim is that they are "Americanizing" it, and it is a claim which, if successful, will incline them, I believe, to use it as an asset in the future, particularly if on the other side the Democrats put forward, as a bid for support, the fact that they stood for a pure, unadulterated League.

What I am fearful of—indeed what those of us who are following this thing very closely are all fearful of—is that the Republicans, if successful in their present policy, will be tempted to definitize their differences with the Democrats by adopting a continuously critical attitude toward the League. They may want to "Americanize" its operation just as they "Americanized" its fundamental constitution, in the belief that such action will be very popular here at home—a belief that is, I fear, altogether too well based. Such a policy on the part of the Republicans might avoid a split which now seems imminent in their party ranks between those who are in favor of reservations and those who would reject the League altogether. I may be wrong in this conjecture of mine. I sincerely hope that I am. Taft believes that once the League is adopted with reservations, the Republicans will play the game. If they do play it, I think it will be because they resist temptation more effectively than political parties generally succeed in doing.

I hate to appear as an apostle of gloom, but I am anxious that you should have as exact a slant on this situation over here as can be obtained.

R. B. F. to Sir Eric Drummond

Washington   January 10, 1920

I cabled you today about the effect of the President's letter to the Jackson Day Dinner, in which he threatened to take the whole issue to the people in the election next fall. I am afraid his illness has so isolated him from the realities of the situation that he does not realize how deeply the distortions and misrepresentations of the Senate debate have stirred up suspicion and fear here in the United States about the purposes of the League of Nations. If this suspicion and misgiving continue to grow, I am not at all certain that the President could win on the issue in November. It would be a difficult issue to put before the country; it couldn't be framed on a "Yes" or "No" basis; and it would be so complicated by extraneous issues and personalities, and by charges and counter-charges, that the people in the end wouldn't be voting on the League of Nations issue at all.

Another thing which obviously doesn't get through to the President, behind the four walls of his sickroom, is that the Armistice was signed a year ago last November, and the people here are heartily tired of the wrangling and the long drawn-out delay in reaching a conclusion to the business. There is a growing disposition to say: "A curse on both your houses." Certainly the President cannot count on keeping alive indefinitely the crusading spirit of the rank and file. The fervor necessary to sustain an exalted mood is waning. You can't keep the public at a high pitch too long.

In all this business we have been shadowed by a double tragedy: first, the attitude of Senator Lodge and his bloc who have seen the League only as a God-given opportunity to crush the President; and second, the illness of Wilson which has robbed us of leadership at a time when we needed it most. The League here in the United States might have survived one or the other tragedy, but it is questionable in my mind whether it can survive both. If Wilson were well—the kind of Wilson we had in Washington for six years—I believe this issue would have been solved long ago. A formula would have been worked out which might not have completely satisfied either side, but which would have saved the League from being scuttled. But with the President completely cut off from contacts and the opportunity for conference, and with a crippling illness which I understand restricts him to the most limited kind of life, this is impossible; and the fight for the League has to be made under circumstances where the commanding officer has fallen desperately wounded on the battlefield and his subordinates are at cross purposes in determining what strategy ought to be followed.

As things are now, we seem to alternate between hope and despair and I fear my letters have reflected this pendulum process. We seize, perhaps too eagerly, on rumors or developments that sound promising, and doubtless we are too depressed by contrary trends. My own position here grows increasingly embarrassing, as well as that of other Americans on the Secretariat. So far, there has been little, if any, public notice of the fact that Americans are now connected with the League, although Senator Borah has threatened to look into the situation. But with the first Council meeting scheduled for a week from this coming Friday, and with the necessity which I assume you face at that time of securing approval for the appointments made under the provisional organization of the League, publicity is bound to be given to the fact that Americans are on the Secretariat, and that one of them is even Under Secretary General, and the President will be open to the charge that he jumped the gun.

I am most anxious not to embarrass him or the cause of the League here at home, and incidentally, I hate this pussyfooting policy which keeps me here in Washington, where I am not wanted, because the only responsible official to whom I can get access—the Secretary of State—is afraid to have me go back to London.

This may sound like a gloomy letter. I hope to have better news to report next time.

League of Nations

R. B. F. to Huntington Gilchrist

Washington   January 5, 1920

I had a batch of letters from you this week, dating all the way from December third to December eighteenth. In two or three of the letters you mention the relationship between Colonel House and the President, and the general attitude of the State Department, and I want to set down everything I know about these matters for your own personal information and guidance. I suggest, however, that if it meets with your concurrence, you read part of this letter to Drummond.

There has been no sharp break between the President and Colonel House. On the other hand, there has been a gradual drifting apart to such an extent that Colonel House is now entirely out of the situation as far as any influence at the White House is concerned. Although several intimate advisers of the President have seen him, Colonel House has not, and his letters to the President remain unanswered. This drifting apart began, I believe, last spring sometime, and was due to several unrelated causes which it is perhaps unnecessary to discuss. The President all along has been very anxious to avoid any appearance of a break, because it is a favorite political charge over here that he throws down his intimate advisers and personal friends whenever he thinks it expedient. It is perfectly true that when the newspaper item of the break was published last August, the President cabled to House expressing his regret. House showed me the cable, and I recall that the President said that he supposed the best way to treat the story was with "silent contempt." Colonel House at that time was very anxious to return home, and the President did not want him to go because he knew that he would be summoned to appear before the Foreign Relations Committee of the Senate. Finally, when the President was taken sick, Colonel House packed up and came anyway. For two months the President was not informed that the Colonel was in this country, and I understand that when he finally learned the news he expressed his dissatisfaction, and particularly his disapproval of the action taken by Colonel House upon landing in New York in writing to Senator Lodge and offering to appear before the Foreign Relations Committee.

Colonel House now, as I say, is entirely out of the situation, and while I would not claim that it is impossible for him to be restored to power when the President gets well, for the present at least he has no more influence than any other man.

This, as you may well imagine, is not at all displeasing to the State Department or to the clique immediately around the President in the White House that has for a long time been jealous of the Colonel's power. In the State Department they make no attempt to hide their pleasure at the undoing of the king's favorite. Colonel House was for months—I might even say years—a thorn in the flesh of the State Department. He never took the trouble to communicate with Secretary Lansing what he was doing, and in reality there were two State Departments—at least there were two agencies handling foreign relations for the United States. Over and over again the State Department people have said to me that they could never get anywhere in reorganizing their office until Colonel House was eliminated from the situation.

Now as to the attitude of Secretary Lansing toward the League, and those of us who are associated with it. Fundamentally, Lansing does not believe in the Covenant. He thinks it is a jumble of legislative, judicial and executive functions, and that it will not work, and he has not hesitated to say so to intimate friends. He believes in a sort of judicial League—an international court with wide powers—a kind of glorified Hague tribunal. In this point of view he concurs with James Brown Scott,[1] and I think that both Lansing and Scott are entirely honest in their convictions. Lansing believes, however, that the Covenant as written should be given a chance to prove itself one way or the

[1] An American international lawyer.

98

other, and this is always the nature of his public utterances. So that in spite of Bullitt's[2] testimony to the effect that Lansing told him that he did not believe in the League, the people are inclined to think that Lansing *does* believe in it; at least they know that he wants it tried.

Lansing's outstanding characteristic, I believe, is timidity. He has almost died of fright during the last three or four months for fear that something would be done by his office that would upset the Senate and lead perhaps to the rejection of the treaty. Lansing does not believe in the treaty any more than he believes in the Covenant, but he realizes that its defeat would leave the world in a state of chaos. This attitude of timidity on his part has embarrassed me tremendously in my relations in Washington. Lansing has taken the position that he could not recognize the existence of even a provisional Secretariat, and he has acted as if he were afraid to see me at the State Department. Letters which I have written on League of Nations stationery have remained unanswered, and I have generally been given to understand that I was a source of embarrassment. While I am sure that he has not wanted me in Washington, least of all has he wanted me to return to London, and in a conversation which he had with Arthur Sweetser the other day he urged him not to go back until the Senate took some action. I think his conversation with Manley Hudson was along much the same line, that is, he wanted Manley to go to Paris and did not want him to go back to the Secretariat even temporarily. This timidity on his part accounts for the almost brutal way in which he treated the International Labor Conference. He would not recognize them, and he would not even admit officially that the delegates were sitting. It further accounts for his insistence that Frank Polk and the American delegation leave Paris at once, in spite of Frank's repeated protests. He was fearful that something would develop in Paris that would upset the apple-cart over here.

2 Yale graduate—a member of the peace delegation at Versailles.

I mention all this in detail because of your recommendation in regard to a liaison between the State Department and the League of Nations in case the Senate failed to ratify or delayed in ratifying. As long as Lansing is in, and the President is sick, I would have absolutely no influence in bringing it about. I am on friendly and even intimate terms with many of Lansing's assistants, but with the Secretary of State himself I can get nowhere.

You will see the unhappy position in which I have been placed. With Colonel House out of it, with the President ill and with Lansing scared to death, I have had literally no place to lay my head. My contacts in Washington would ordinarily be directly with the President, whom I have known for many years; but since he was taken sick only two or three people have seen him, and I, naturally enough, have not been one of them. I of course have cordial relations with the White House crowd, but that doesn't get one very far. Until the situation in the Senate clears up, I do not look for any happier condition.

I have written at length because I want you to understand intimately just what this situation is over here. Of course, just as soon as the Republicans in the Senate make up their minds what they are going to do, the situation will clear up.

R. B. F. to his father, Frank S. Fosdick

Washington   January 10, 1920

To have to stand by and see the wrong thing done when the right thing seems so obvious is exhausting business. Those dreadful memories of dead men hanging on barbed wire won't let me sleep. Must this thing happen again?

I keep saying to myself: "You have this thing out of perspective. Whether we join the League or not isn't as important as you imagine." But it doesn't do any good. I *know* it is important. It is perhaps the single important decision of our generation. Of course, the League may not work, but it is the only thing that stands between us and another war—the only hope we have, frail as it may be. Its opponents offer no alternatives. They are intent on killing *this* plan, but they haven't a single idea to put in its place; and as Wilson said out West: "The world cannot breathe in an atmosphere of negations."

R. B. F. to Sir Eric Drummond

Washington   January 17, 1920

I cabled you today as follows:

"I am sincerely sorry that the President's invitation to the Powers to attend the first meeting of the Council of the League was issued through diplomatic channels instead of through the Secretary General. At the last moment there was some feeling at the State Department that there was not time enough to send the invitation through the Secretary General. I am writing in more detail."

The "time" argument had something to do with the situation—that is Lansing felt that if the invitation went through the Secretary General's office it might not give enough time to the Powers, and that rather than risk any delay it would be better to send the matter through the usual diplomatic channels. I am bound to confess, however, that this was not the real reason. Lansing, as I think I have told you before, doesn't really believe in the League of Nations and is entirely out of sympathy with our whole plan. He is not going to play any more closely with us than he absolutely has to. In the matter of the invitations, the President was not and could not, of course, be consulted, and Lansing had the thing his own way. It is a most deplorable situation, but until the President gets better or some shift is made in the State Department, I do not see any chance of changing it.

The news of the first meeting of the Council yesterday is given space in today's newspapers here. Sweetser and I both feel that if the League could start off with a flourish as a going organization and with a full agenda, it would be better

101

than to have it start off in a hesitating sort of way. I think it would make a very good impression here if the League should begin to function with prestige and authority, starting out on plans for disarmament, international court, and all the humanitarian measures that are connected with the program. It would make Americans feel tremendously uncomfortable if they realized that big matters like these were afoot in which they had no part. That was why Sweetser and I cabled you as we did the other day. Personally, I believe the time for pussy footing is over, and I think that you can safely, as far as the situation over here is concerned, give all manner of publicity to the plans and personnel of the Secretariat.

The Senate situation seems to be moving slowly toward a possible compromise. At the same time, powerful forces are being brought to bear on the President to get him to meet the compromise half way. I have known him to withstand equally powerful influences before, and he may do it again. So that things are not much different than they were a week ago when I wrote you. On the other hand, I cannot help feeling, with no particular reason for it, that the situation is a little brighter.

Please give my warm regards to my associates in London. To be out of the situation now that the League is really going, is most galling.

R. B. F. to President Wilson

Washington   January 14, 1920

As you will recall, Sir Eric Drummond last June appointed me Under Secretary General of the provisional organization of the League of Nations. In this capacity I worked with him in London until October, when I returned to represent him at the meeting of the International Labor Conference here in Washington. When the Conference completed its work and my duties in connection therewith were finished, I did not go back to London because I was afraid that with the critical condition existing in the Senate, any publicity as to the connection of an American with the League might prove harmful. This appeared, too, to be the judgment of Secretary Lansing. During the interim, therefore, I have endeavored to keep Sir Eric Drummond in intimate touch with the situation in America, so that he and his associates could gauge the drift of events.

My connection with the Secretariat has consequently been kept quiet, and as a result my position has been too much that of a "pussy footer" to be comfortable. The fact that my salary has been paid from moneys contributed to the League by the French, Belgian and English governments, whereas America has made no contribution, has added decidedly to my feeling of embarrassment. However, Sir Eric Drummond has been anxious that I should stay on, and has refused to consider my offer of resignation unless I should press it for reasons arising out of the situation in America.

I feel, however, that with the League holding its first Council meeting this coming Friday, my position will be increasingly embarrassing. It is entirely possible that some announcement will be made from Paris as to the personnel of the Secretariat, and I am not at all sure what the effect of such an announcement will be in the Senate. What would you advise me to do? Now that the League has become a going concern rather than a provisional organization, will my continued connection with the Secretariat jeopardize the cause? Am I justified in accepting a salary from a fund to which America has not contributed? I may say in this connection, perhaps, that I accepted the position last June only because I felt that it was an obligation from which I could not conscientiously escape. Resignation would relieve me of the burden of personal sacrifice which I have been obliged to make. On the other hand, because I believe the League of Nations is the most challenging cause which has been presented to my generation, I am anxious to serve it to the limit of my ability.

There are, perhaps, half a dozen other Americans on the Secretariat who find themselves in a similar position. Mr. Arthur Sweetser, who is attached to the Public Information Section of the Secretariat, is with me here in Washington. Captain Gilchrist, my assistant, is in London with Sir Eric Drummond. The other Americans actively serving on the Secretariat at present are Manley Hudson, attached to the Legal Section, Miss Florence Wilson, Assistant Librarian, Howard Huston, Establishment Officer, and one or two others in positions of lesser importance.

I have naturally hesitated to intrude on your illness with such a detail as this, but the question concerns others than myself, and may have important consequences. May I take this opportunity, as one who has been proud to call himself your friend and follower from old Princeton days, to express the wish, shared, I believe, by the entire world that your return to health and vigor may not be delayed.

J. P. Tumulty[1] to R. B. F.

Washington   January 16, 1920

The President has carefully read your letter of the 14th of January, and has asked me to say to you that he feels he cannot decide the question it contains as he thinks it is one which should be left to you and the gentlemen associated with you to take counsel together and determine in concert what it is right to do.

R. B. F. to J. P. Tumulty

Washington   January 19, 1920

I have your letter of January 16th in reply to my letter to the President of the 14th. Under the circumstances I feel that there is but one thing for me to do, and that is to tender my resignation as Under Secretary General of the League.

[1] Joseph Tumulty was secretary to Woodrow Wilson during his years at the White House.

This is the advice that I get from all the President's friends with whom I have talked. You will understand, I am sure, that the question is not in any sense a personal one. I feel that my position as Under Secretary General exposes the League to the possibility of an attack, which at the present critical juncture might do great harm, and I do not believe that I ought myself to assume the responsibility of continuing in a relationship which might help further to imperil the cause. I have therefore cabled my resignation to Sir Eric Drummond, and I am enclosing a copy of it herewith.

Tumulty to R. B. F.

Washington   January 21, 1920

It was with regret that I received your letter of the 19th of January, telling me that you had tendered your resignation as Under Secretary General of the League of Nations. However I understand your position.

R. B. F.'s Statement to the Press

Washington   January 19, 1920

. . . . Now that the League of Nations is no longer a provisional organization, but has become established as a going concern, the continued lack of decision as to America's course places me personally in a position of peculiar embarrassment. In order, therefore, to avoid any confusion or misunderstanding as to my position as Under Secretary General of the League, it seems best for me to tender my resignation. I do this with deep regret because I do not like to appear to be abandoning those with whom I have been associated for the past few months just at the moment when their responsibilities and opportunities are becoming real. The League is now approaching the point where it can begin to carry out the world's hopes for disarmament, arbitration, the protection of backward people, the furthering of international health projects and all the other humanitarian issues upon which we have been working for the past six months. I feel sure, however, that you will appreciate the reasons which have led up to my decision and will recognize that if as an American I now feel forced to withdraw from official connection with the Secretariat, it is not for lack of faith in the League.

R. B. F. to Colonel House

Washington   January 19, 1920

I have today cabled to Sir Eric Drummond my resignation as Under Secretary General.

I have been greatly troubled, as you know, over the situation of peculiar embarrassment in which I found myself by reason of the fact that America had not joined the League. Last Friday I dropped into the White House to see Tumulty, and when I mentioned the matter to him he expressed his belief that the President was not aware of the fact that there were any Americans still connected with the Secretariat. He thought that it would be well, therefore, to put the whole thing up to the President in a letter, and ask his advice. This I did. I told the President fully just what the situation was, and asked him whether he thought I ought to resign or continue. Two days later I had the following letter from Tumulty: [text of letter of January 16, 1920] Upon receipt of this letter I did not feel that without the positive support of the President I could myself assume the responsibility of continuing in the position of Under Secretary General. Frank Polk and Newton Baker both concurred in this opinion, and I thereupon sent the following cablegram to Drummond: [text of R.B.F.'s statement to the Press January 19, 1920].

It is not necessary for me to tell you that I shall never regret the opportunity which I have had to serve the League of Nations, even in the small part which I have played in the last six months. I am afraid we have lost the fight, but it has been a fight well worth making and I am proud to have had a share in it. For all your friendly counsel and guidance I can never be sufficiently grateful. It has been a privilege to have worked in this thing, if only to have been associated with you.

R. B. F. to Sir Eric Drummond

Washington   January 19, 1920

I sent you today the following by cable: [text of R.B.F.'s statement to the Press, January 19, 1920]. There is little that I can add to what I have said above. My position here, as you know, has been embarrassing to the extreme. After the treaty was ratified and the League held its first meeting, it became intolerable. I felt that I was working in a vacuum, and my inability to establish contact either at the State Department or in the White House led to my final decision. With the League a going concern and the United States not represented, I did not feel that without the positive support of some government authority I could myself assume the responsibility of continuing in my relationship to the Secretariat.

You know, I am sure, the reluctance with which I have taken this step. I postponed it until the last possible moment, feeling that perhaps something might develop which would obviate its necessity. More than anything else I want to avoid the appearance of abandoning in a light and irresponsible fashion the cause for which so many sacrifices have already been made, and the colleagues in London with whom I have been associated on such intimate terms.

I am not saying goodbye because I want very much to return to London at an early date to settle up my affairs at Sunderland House, and to tell you personally of my satisfaction in having had an opportunity to serve the League, even in the small part which I have played in the last six months.

R. B. F. to Huntington Gilchrist

Washington   January 19, 1920

I sent you today the following cable:

"Matters reached a sudden crisis here in Washington to-day, which makes it advisable for me to tender my resignation as Under Secretary General. I am confident in view of the relations between the Senate and the White House that this step is wise. It has the concurrence of Polk, Baker and others with whom I have been in intimate contact. It need not necessarily affect the relations to the Secretariat of yourself, Hudson, Sweetser or any of the others. In fact, I see no reason from this distance why any of you should resign unless the delay in the Senate becomes unduly prolonged. My own position is affected solely because of the rank which I hold on the Secretariat, but my action need not be taken as a precedent for others. My advice would be that you hang on for at least two or three weeks longer to see what the Senate is going to do. This is Sweetser's decision for himself. He will remain on for perhaps a month to finish the work on the handbook upon which he is now engaged. The text of my resignation to Drummond will appear in the press. If it meets with Drummond's concurrence, I should like to return to London for a few days to clear up my affairs at Sunderland House. In the meantime please continue communications and let us have all the news as before."

I think this tells most of the story, but perhaps I can elaborate a bit. As you know, my position here has been increasingly embarrassing, because with Colonel House out of favor, with Secretary Lansing opposed to the League, and with the President ill, I have been suspended in a vacuum. Last Friday I had a long talk with Tumulty, and to my great amazement he expressed the belief that the President did not know that there were Americans aside from myself serving on the Secretariat. At his suggestion I wrote to the

President a long letter in which I outlined the whole situation and asked his opinion as to what I should do. In reply I had the following letter from Mr. Tumulty: [text of letter of January 16, 1920]. Under the circumstances I did not feel that without the support of the President I could myself assume the responsibility of continuing in the position of Under Secretary General. The question was not a personal one in any sense; it involved a policy which might possibly jeopardize the adherence of the United States to the League, and when the President passed the buck back to me I felt that there was but one thing for me to do. I was confirmed in this belief by the advice of Polk and Baker. Colonel House was in the south, so I could not get to him, but I am confident that he would have given the same advice.

As I told you in my cable, I do not believe that this decision necessarily affects your position or the position of the others on the Secretariat. It was the rank "Under Secretary General" which has been the danger point right along. On the other hand, I do not feel that you and the others can continue on this proposition indefinitely, although I do not believe that in any event the decision or lack of decision of the Senate ought necessarily to affect Miss Wilson's position, or Huston's, or the position of any of the translators, etc., who are doing technical, routine work. Sweetser has decided to stay on for two or three weeks longer, as he wants to finish a handbook upon which he is now working. Hudson, I presume, has already transferred his activities to Paris so that he is not necessarily concerned. If I were you, I would stay on for two or three weeks until the decision of the United States becomes more clearly outlined. I am under the impression that perhaps we owe this to Drummond, who ought to have some continuous contact with the United States during this critical period. I shall be right here in Washington so that we can keep up the same system of communication that we have had. In spite of the fact that I have resigned, I see no reason why I should not continue to function over here as I have right along, insofar as I can be of any assistance to those in London.

The text of my resignation to Drummond will go out over the Associated Press wires tonight. I think it will make good propaganda, and I shall follow it up with several interviews of a kind that I could not give while I was on the League. I really think that we can make the resignation a point of attack on the general condition of apathy around the country, and we are going to work it for all that it is worth.

I confess, however, I have not much hope about the final result because the proceedings in the Senate are dragging unconscionably, and if any result is achieved I am very, very fearful that it will be one which will not be acceptable to the President. The President's mood has not changed, and the incursion of Bryan has hindered rather than helped.

Altogether, it is a sorry, agonizing mess, and as an American I hang my head in shame. My only satisfaction in resigning is that it releases me from the burden of silence. I can now speak my faith before the world. I shall do it in as loud and eloquent tones as I can employ.

I hope soon to come to London—just how soon I cannot say. The sailings in the next three or four weeks do not seem to be particularly propitious, but I should think that I might come over sometime in February, if this suits Drummond's ideas.

Huntington Gilchrist to R. B. F.

Paris   January 22, 1920

The announcement of your resignation reached us first through the morning papers yesterday and caused considerable consternation. There are only a few of us left in Paris, but the general impression here is that your decision is very much to be regretted and is really unfortunate from the standpoint of the interests of the League and the Secretariat.

Comert[1] felt this very strongly, as he thinks that the national position which a member of the Secretariat may hold can easily be over-emphasized. Of course, we all feel that it is impossible to express any opinion with regard to what action might be required by the political situation in Washington, and no one questions your judgment as to that. Several people have said, however, that they wished you had come back to Europe for regular work with the Secretariat, and if this course had been followed, this regrettable resignation would not have been necessary, because in Europe the Americans connected with the League cannot feel the embarrassment which you mention in your cable. The Paris edition of the *New York Herald* and the *Chicago Tribune* gave a front page notice of the resignation and the London *Times* mentioned it in the general dispatch on the Treaty situation in Washington. The text of your communication reached us during the morning, but as it was evidently written for the Press, it did not enlighten us very much as to your real feeling about the relationship between Americans and the Secretariat. Late in the day came your message to me, which cleared up the situation considerably. I wish, however, that we did know a little more definitely what crisis caused you to take your final decision. I had dinner with Drummond last night, and we went over the best kind of reply which could be sent. Drummond said that he wished you had cabled over the reply which you want (!) as it is very difficult to know what would carry best in the Press. I intended to return to London with Drummond last night to talk things over with Davis,[2] and I shall do that on Friday. Drummond has said two or three times lately that he really must have someone to assist him in

[1] A brilliant French journalist, Pierre Comert was attached to the French delegation at the Treaty of Versailles. Later he became Director of the Press and Information Section of the League of Nations.

[2] John W. Davis was Solicitor General of the United States Supreme Court from 1913 to 1918. He later served as the American Ambassador to the Court of St. James from 1918-1921. Nominated for President of the United States on the Democratic ticket in 1924, he was defeated by Calvin Coolidge.

handling such questions as you and he were accustomed to go over together last summer and last fall. He is most enthusiastic about the way in which Monnet has organized the French Government for liaison with the League, but Monnet does not enjoy looking over papers and giving the careful consideration to some of the memoranda and specific problems which are presented for the opinion of and action by the Secretary-General. Drummond feels very much the need of your assistance in that direction, and if he can not expect your co-operation before long, he feels that he must make plans to get someone else to assist him in that way. I hope very much that you will be able to come back in the very immediate future, and that before you have been in Europe long the Senate situation will be such that you can join the Secretariat again. . . . .

Manley Hudson to R. B. F.

Paris   January 23, 1920

We were exceedingly disappointed to learn of your resignation. The news first came in the *New York Herald* and was confirmed during the day by your cable to Drummond. Drummond hardly knew how to take your cable. I think his decision when he left night before last for London was that he would accept your resignation, but no appointment of your successor would be made until you have a chance to come back if you wish. I take this to be what you wanted from your cable, and Drummond is most desirous to do exactly what you want done. Many of the people here have expressed regret that you should have found it necessary to resign. I take it that some development of the personal situation in Washington made it necessary in your mind.

My hopes for the United States ratification before March 1st are not so high as they were. I hardly see how it is possible for the politicians to let the President put the Treaty issue into the campaign. Surely it will not be possible unless the President keeps wholly out of touch with the political managers. The feeling in France is one of great bitterness towards the United States. The people cannot understand our political situation at all. Even many of the British take the same view. . . . .

R. B. F. to Sir Eric Drummond

Washington   January 27, 1920

I have just received your cable of January 23rd accepting my resignation as Under Secretary General. It was good of you to express yourself so generously, and I appreciate it very much. I have not made the cable public because I think that the full effect of the situation was obtained by the publication of my own cable to you. Judging from the newspapers and from such comments as I have heard, the resignation helped to emphasize the continued delay and the inability of the United States even to assist in plans for the preparation of a world order. Of course, some of the Republican papers took occasion to hammer me pretty hard, notably the *Chicago Tribune*, but that doesn't count for much. I am confident that my resignation was a wise step. All the President's friends approve it, and men like Taft and Hoover seem to think that under the circumstances it was the only thing to do.

The situation today looks pretty gloomy as far as the participation of the United States is concerned. The small committee in the Senate which has been working on a compromise crashed last night on Article X, just as we expected they would, and the plans which seemed to hold a ray of hope have fallen to the ground. The difficulty is that any compromise on the reservation on Article X, or on the Monroe Doctrine would split the Republican party in two, and Lodge is forced by the interests of party preservation to adhere to his doctrine of no compromise. The President, I am afraid, is almost equally firm for no compromise on the other side, although we have been getting more encouraging reports lately as to his attitude.

In Gilchrist's cable to me he expressed for you and Monnet the hope that my separation would be a temporary one only. The difficulty with the position is just this: If the United States accedes, it will accede only on the basis of certain reservations which must be accepted by the Senate and the President. So far there has been no movement to alter the wording of reservation number seven, and I do not believe that any movement will be made in that direction, inasmuch as this particular reservation seems to be fairly popular around the country. So that I am afraid that if the President and the Senate get together at all, the seventh reservation will remain untouched. The last phrase of this reservation reads as follows: "No citizen of the United States shall be selected or appointed as a member of said commissions, committees, tribunals, courts, councils, or conferences except with the approval of the Senate of the United States." The Solicitor of the State Department and all the legal authorities that I have consulted in Washington hold that this affects my position on the Secretariat, and that I could not be appointed except with the approval of the Senate. So that even if we assume that the President and the Senate find some basis upon which to get together, I do not see how I could be appointed without the approval of the Senate. Personally, I do not believe that I could secure the approval of the Senate in a thousand years, at least not of this Senate.

I mention this point, not that it has any particular importance, but only because of the message which you and Monnet sent me through Gilchrist. There are plenty of Americans who can serve as Under Secretary General more acceptably than I, and the personal question has no proper place in the situation.

As I cabled the other day, I want to come to London to straighten out my affairs over there, and I hope that before this letter reaches you I shall be on the ocean. My plans are a bit uncertain, and so far I have found so much to do in connection with the League—particularly since my resignation went in—that I do not know exactly when I can get away. Sweetser and I are carrying on a propaganda which I think is helping some, although the situation has almost entirely gotten beyond the influence of argument or reason. ....

R. B. F. to Huntington Gilchrist

Washington   January 28, 1920

I have your letter of January 7th in which you mention the advisability of Lord Robert Cecil coming to America to tour the country for the League. No man is better fitted for this task than Lord Robert Cecil, and no man's word would be more eagerly awaited or more thoroughly respected. He is known as a liberal, and I am confident that he would have a cordial reception. On the other hand, with the situation as it is just now, any Englishman who comes over here to urge the adhesion of the United States to the League is going to do more harm than good. Indeed, he will do a terrible amount of harm, because all sorts of antagonistic influences such as the Hearst newspapers, the Irish propagandists, etc., are continually harping on the belief that Great Britain is merely using America as a cat's-paw to play her own imperialistic games. I am amazed at the extent of anti-British feeling in this country. This morning, for example, Hearst begins an attack on Lord Grey, alleging that Grey was present at the dinner which Colonel House gave to launch the boom of Hoover for President. The story is false from start of finish, but that will not prevent Hearst from printing it, nor will it prevent thousands of Americans from believing it. America is in a mood now where she will believe anything bad about anybody, and she is prepared to believe the worst about Englishmen. No, Lord Robert Cecil should not come over now, and I doubt whether he should come before the campaign next fall, that is, if he wants to help the League.

R. B. F. to Mrs. Raymond Fosdick

Washington   January 30, 1920

. . . . On the whole I think the newspapers have treated my resignation fairly. And I think it helped to underscore the isolation of America—the fact that we now stand alone against the world. Of course some of the Republican papers couldn't resist the opportunity to take an editorial poke at me, but it was obvious that the President was the target—and not me. As I expected, the ineffable *Chicago Tribune* took a lusty swing at me, saying that "when the other young men went to war Mr. Fosdick organized a movement which gave him a remunerative, comfortable, and safe position which catered to his sense of self-gratification."

Just for fun, I showed the editorial to Newton Baker. He read it through slowly and carefully without saying a word. Then he deliberately filled his pipe, put his feet on his desk, and after a couple of husky puffs he said rather grimly: "Raymond, I wish now that as a youth I had learned to swear." Wasn't that just like him?

R. B. F.'s Statement to the *New York Times*

Washington   February 8, 1920

. . . . Another misconception which seems everywhere to be prevalent is that the League is a sort of super-government and that there is something in the Covenant which subtly transfers authority in our national concerns from Washington to Geneva. This belief is spread by the statements and speeches of men like Senator Johnson and Senator Borah. The out-and-out opponents of the League are basing their position on the necessity of preserving nationalism from internationalism, and of protecting Washington from the control of Geneva.

Now it seems very strange that no such idea has developed in England or France. Both these countries now are experiencing a recrudescence of nationalism just as real and determined as anything we know in America. There are powerful movements in each country to preserve England for the English and France for the French, and to cut loose from foreign influences; and yet in neither country is there any idea that adherence to the League involves a surrender of sovereignty. If the British thought for one minute that the League was merely a veiled attempt to transfer authority away from Westminster, they would be the first to kick over the traces, for I believe there are no people as jealous of their own rights and institutions as the English.

As a matter of fact, the flaming appeals of Senators Borah and Johnson are absolutely false, and it is sometimes difficult to believe that they are sincere. Anyone who has read the Covenant knows that the government of the League is committed primarily into the hands of a small executive body of nine members called the Council. Assisting the Council in a more or less advisory capacity is a much larger body, called the Assembly, but the actual administration is in the hands of this small committee of nine. On this committee, or Council, are the representatives of the five allied and associated powers, and of four smaller powers. Under the Covenant, the United States will always be a member of the Council. Under the Covenant, too, the decisions of the Council have to be unanimous in all matters that relate to peace or war or the methods by which the judgment of the world is put into effect. The United States has an absolute veto power on any move or motion it does not like. At any time it can stop anything that it does not agree with. Senator Johnson talks about our being under compulsion to send over our boys to die on the battlefields of Europe. This compulsion exists only in Senator Johnson's mind. The vote of the American member on the Council against sending United States troops overseas or anywhere else, would, under Article V of the Covenant, absolutely defeat it. We can exercise a complete control not only over the policies of the League, but over the methods by which those policies are put into effect.

Legitimate criticism can be directed against the League of Nations, not because it is a super-state—for it is not—but because in order to preserve the sovereignty of its constituent members, it had to be weakened almost to the point of impotence. It was a choice between a sacrifice of national sovereignty and a sacrifice of power, and the framers of the Covenant chose the latter. If the League breaks down it will not be because it is a super-state, but because in trying to avoid being a super-state, it decentralized its authority beyond the possibility of positive action and control.

R. B. F. to Sir Eric Drummond

Washington February 13, 1920

After much backing and filling, the Treaty is again before the Senate, and we are now in hopes that some definite action will be taken.[1] Lodge, however, has added a new difficulty by bringing in a reservation on Article X that is stronger than the reservation first proposed, and just at this writing the Democrats are threatening to kick over the traces. The irreconcilables are planning a new line of attack on the Treaty, based on the reparations clauses, and the total disregard of President Wilson's fourteen points. Up to this time they have hesitated to launch this attack because it savored of pro-Germanism and the country was in too excited and illiberal a mood to stand for it. They feel now, however, that such an attack is possible and that it stands a good chance of gaining public support among the liberal and labor elements. In this they have the powerful backing of Keynes' book, which has made and is making a profound impression in America.[2] It is discussed everywhere, and while David Hunter Miller[3] has attempted to answer it in the press, the answers have been rather feeble and futile.

---

[1] On February 10, 1920, Senator Lodge reported the Treaty back to the Senate and there ensued five weeks of further debate, in which the reservations were made more objectionable to the President.

[2] *The Economic Consequences of the Peace.*

[3] Legal adviser to Colonel House.

However, I do not believe that the irreconcilables will be successful in upsetting the situation by this line of attack, principally for the reason that liberalism is not in the saddle in the United States just now, and liberal opinion here is almost inarticulate. If the difficulty in regard to Article X can be bridged, I look to see the Treaty ratified in about a month, with reservations substantially those reported out by the Lodge committee three months ago. Of course, there is many a slip twixt the cup and the lip, and we cannot tell what unforeseen obstacles may un-horse us, but I am more optimistic about the situation than I have been before. Sweetser and I have been carrying on a campaign of publicity which I think has helped materially. It was for that reason that I did not take as early a boat as I at first intended, and now I find that I can probably get no accommodations before the *Imperator*, which leaves New York on March sixth. I have been trying for the *Lapland* on February twenty-fifth, but I understand it is out of the question, as the competition for space is unprecedented.

As I told you in a letter the other day, the new reservations still maintain the principle that United States citizens are ineligible to serve on any agency set up by the Treaty without the consent of the Senate, and this is held to affect appointments to the Secretariat. For that reason, I do not believe that there is any possibility of my returning to my position as Under Secretary General, because I do not think I could obtain the necessary support in the Senate. My affiliations with the President and the Secretary of War, would, I am afraid, be enough to defeat me, quite apart from the fact that my previous connection with the League of Nations during a time when America had not ratified, would be a decided handicap. We had hoped that some change would be made in the reservation regarding appointments, excepting the Secretariat from its scope—and I believe that Sweetser cabled you the other day to this effect; but the reservation as introduced day before yesterday was as strong as ever, and I do not look for any change in it.

I cannot tell you how irritating it has been to be put in the position of abandoning ship at a time when all hands are needed. Gilchrist writes that you feel very much the necessity of having someone to assist you in the work of general administration, and under ordinary circumstances I should hope that the American Under Secretary General, whoever he may be, could fill this position. It seems unfair, however, with all the burdens under which you are now laboring, to ask you to wait until America has ratified. My advice would be, therefore, if the burden becomes too great, not to hesitate to make any arrangements that are necessary. The work of the League cannot wait on America's dilly-dallying.

I gathered, too, from what Gilchrist wrote me the other day, that some regret had been expressed that I had not returned to Europe earlier, on the theory that no embarrassment would have arisen over there in connection with my association with the League. The difficulty was that Secretary Lansing, and in fact the whole State Department, were opposed to this course, and were particularly anxious that I should not return because of the attention which it might focus on the fact that Americans were connected with the Secretariat, although the Senate had not yet ratified. I held on as long as I could in the anomalous position in which I found myself, and resigned only when I found that I did not even have the support of the President in staying on.

Of course, there are many, many things that I want to talk with you about that I cannot write, and that is chiefly why I am anxious to return now. I am sorry to have been delayed, but I think in the last three weeks I have been able to be of greater service to the League here than I would have been over there, although it would be a great convenience if I could get away now instead of waiting until March sixth. However, it is possible that some break will occur in shipping schedules to allow me to embark earlier.

R. B. F. to Sir Eric Drummond (cablegram)

Washington   February 20, 1920

Matters are going from bad to worse and it begins to look now as if the ratification of the Treaty by the Senate would be indefinitely postponed. The resignation of Lansing has greatly embarrassed the situation, and the attempted settlement of the Fiume incident on the basis of the Pact of London has added to the complication. Public interest in the problem is distinctly growing weaker. The decision yesterday in the Senate to substitute the Railroad Bill for the Peace Treaty as the order of the day, has produced hardly a ripple of protest from the newspapers. The belief seems to be gaining ground that the European situation is perhaps so chaotic that America better steer clear. On the other hand, this has not become as yet a clearly defined attitude, although it is being given much impetus by Keynes' book and the attacks of the Liberals. Public opinion is so confused and the cross currents are so many and varied, that general statements about it are difficult to make. In any event, the League of Nations is bound to come up as an issue in the political campaign next Fall, regardless of any action that the Senate may take. I am still planning to sail on the "Imperator" on March sixth unless you tell me you think it unnecessary or inadvisable. . . . .

R. B. F. to Frank Polk[1]

Washington   March 3, 1920

I telephoned your office yesterday in Washington and talked with your secretary about my trip overseas. I am sailing Saturday on the *Imperator* to finish up some odds and ends of work at Sunderland House with the League of Nations. I shall be there only two weeks, and shall be back in a month. I was anxious that you should understand just what the purpose of my trip is, because some inquiry might

---

[1] Acting Secretary of State.

be made about it. In connection with the development of the League's machinery, I had three or four special problems that I was working out, and Drummond was anxious to have me come back and tie the whole thing up before I left for keeps. Your secretary told me that he would explain the situation to you, and that you would telephone if there was any question in your mind about it. . . . .

R. B. F. to Mrs. Raymond Fosdick

March 11, 1920   On board S.S. *Imperator*

I remember writing you nine months ago from the *Aquitania* when I was going over to take on the new job. The hope was so real and the chance for a decent world seemed so vivid and tangible! And now it is all washed up and the adventure is gone. I don't care about myself in this business, as you know. I shall certainly be happier practicing law at home than living a lonely life in Europe. And I have never had any illusions of special competence for the job; and the title *Under Secretary General* has always seemed a bit grandiose.

But I do care deeply and, I confess, passionately, about America's desertion and the chance we've missed to make this world a fit place to live in instead of a place to fight in. We had the most unique opportunity that ever came to any generation, and we weren't wise enough to see it or big enough to take it.

R. B. F. to his brother, Harry Emerson Fosdick

London   March 29, 1920

It's hard to be an American in Europe these days—hard to hold your chin up. For we have to face this inescapable fact: We left Europe in the lurch in the middle of the game after imposing on her our ideas and our procedures. In a single year we have lost the confidence and affection of the people of all nations—people who believed that under our leadership this war-weary world would find a way out. We didn't lose the position; we deliberately threw it away. We let cynicism and lies and partisan politics get the better of us, and we chucked the League out of the window to satisfy a miserable political quarrel. . . . Our generation in America has betrayed its own children and the blood of the next war is on our hands.

R. B. F. to Mrs. Raymond Fosdick

London   March 30, 1920

Before I left America, people kept saying: "What a tragedy for Wilson!" But nobody need be concerned about Wilson! History will vindicate him and will place him among its prophets and heroes. He dared and apparently failed, but that has been the fate of many men whose memories the world reveres. Most generations stone their prophets. This is not Wilson's tragedy. It is America's tragedy. It is the tragedy of the next generation.

R. B. F. to Sir Eric Drummond

April 9, 1920   On board S.S. *Baltic*

I want once again to thank you for your generous understanding during these difficult and humiliating days. We Americans on the Secretariat will not soon forget it. It has been a privilege to be associated with you, and if for reasons beyond our control some of us must now leave the work, we take with us the proud memory of a gallant beginning in a great cause under your leadership.

And the cause is by no means lost. Rather the fight has just begun—a more difficult fight than we imagined ten months ago. In the United States the issue never can be settled until it is settled right. I am an American and I want to see my pride in belonging to America justified by her willing acceptance of the role she must play if the world is to be saved from shipwreck. For of this I am convinced: If through ill will or ignorance or apathy we fumble this chance to establish a definitized system of international relationships, another generation will wade through agony and blood before the chance comes again.

Once more let me thank you for your words, both expressed and unexpressed, during these dark days through which we have lived together.

My loyal and affectionate greetings to you and all my associates on the Secretariat.

R. B. F.'s Statement to the Press on Returning from London

New York   April 11, 1920

In spite of the refusal of the United States to join the compact, the League of Nations is now a going concern. Its machinery is practically completed, its finances are ample, and it is beginning to make itself felt in international affairs. All the countries that were neutral during the war have joined, including Spain, Norway, Sweden, Denmark and Switzerland. Every country in South America, except Ecuador, is now a member of the League. Even the two countries that have been more or less under our particular care—Liberia and Panama—have not waited for the United States, but have joined with the others. Outside of Russia and the Central Empires of Europe, Roumania and Jugo Slavia are the only important countries that have not yet come in, and their accession is now merely a matter of weeks. China's accession is included in the Austrian treaty which will shortly be signed.

In other words, the League of Nations is a world-alliance. It includes Asia and Africa as well as Europe—the Western hemisphere as well as the Eastern hemisphere. It has drawn to itself Canada to the north of us and all of South America on our southern boundary. Financial and trade agreements will bring its members into increasingly closer relationships. Treaties and conventions on such subjects as currency, food, raw materials, trade combinations, the flow of commerce, markets, etc., will add to its solidarity and cohesiveness.

Already a financial and economic conference of the members of the League has been summoned to meet in May. South America is enthusiastically participating, and the forthcoming visit there of the King of Spain is significant of the new political and economic ties between our southern neighbors and Europe.

Meanwhile the United States stands aloof. Our isolation is complete and we face the rest of the world in alliance. It is foolish to assume that the situation has no elements of danger in it for us. Our position is one of peril, a fact that is evidently realized in Washington, judging from the plans that are being laid for the biggest navy in the world. The price of our isolation will be armaments.

For it must not be forgotten that the ghastly business in Washington has left us without a friend anywhere. All that we won during the war we have deliberately thrown away. The influence that we had, our position of leadership, the affection in which everything relating to America was held, have all gone by the board. The last three months have brought a complete change of opinion. Only one who has been in Europe recently can realize the depth and bitterness of the feeling against us. We are regarded as a race of "quitters" and our professions of idealism and disinterestedness are marked down for sham and hypocrisy. We started something that we later refused to see through. We left Europe in the lurch in the middle of the game, after imposing on her our rules and procedure. We threw the League out of the window to satisfy a miserable political quarrel. That is the way Europe looks at it. A high French official put the situation to me as follows: "There was a time when the word 'American' almost brought tears to the eyes of every Frenchman, when the fact that an article was made in America guaranteed it a market with us. Not now and never again!"

Personally I believe that this wave of intense bitterness will pass. But the position of the United States outside the League will always be one of danger. We are the richest country in the world while Europe is bankrupt. We have raw materials in abundance while parts of Europe are starving. The world's gold supply is flowing steadily in our direction. Europe's debt to us amounts to over ten billion dollars. There is no relation more dangerous to friendship than that of creditor and debtor. The obvious inability of Germany to pay the large indemnities that were expected will add an additional strain to the relationship, because it will throw on the Allies most of the burden of paying for the war. As a member of the League the United States could help enormously to tide over a difficult and dangerous period, to introduce sane and steadying counsels into the tangled affairs of Europe, and to reestablish the economic and industrial life of the world. If she stays outside the League and cuts herself off from any relationship with other nations except that of creditor, she must be prepared to arm to the teeth as the price of safety against a world in alliance.

R. B. F. to the *New York Times*

New York   September 1, 1920

Senator Harding pronounces the League of Nations "a failure and a wreck beyond the possibility of repair," and Senator Lodge characterizes it as "a battered hulk."

What are the facts?

1. The League of Nations is now composed of thirty-nine member-nations, representing seven-eighths of the people of the globe. Practically all the nations of the world have joined it except the United States, Russia, Mexico and the ex-enemy countries. It seems probable that Germany and Austria will be admitted at the meeting of the Assembly of the League to be held at Geneva in November. . . .

2. The plans for a permanent court of international justice have been completed and are ready for submission to the Assembly of the League at its meeting in November. Mr. Root served as a member of this particular subdivision of the League's activity. . . .

3. Single-handed in Poland, with funds provided by its

members, the League is fighting the typhus epidemic, doing its best to keep back from the rest of the world the flood of this fearful scourge. The estimated cost of this work is $15,000,000. The United States has no part in the financing. . . .

4. The League has established an International Health Office, a bureau to fight the international exploitation of opium and other drugs, and a division to suppress the international trade in women and girls.

These points represent some of the main activities of the League in the seven months of its existence. It is far from "wrecked." It is going ahead most courageously, rapidly organizing its work, regardless of the United States. We cannot destroy it, nor can we substitute another league in its place. Indeed, the latter contention is the sheerest absurdity. We have only two choices: to stay outside of a community of nations organized for cooperation and peace and thereby lose our whole place in the world, or to come into the League, with reservations if we think necessary, and put our shoulder to the wheel in all those great movements for which American foreign policy has always stood.

R. B. F. to Dr. Abraham Flexner

New York   October 11, 1920

No, you are wrong. We are out of the League because the Republicans took advantage of Wilson's tactlessness to make party capital out of. It seems to me you put the cart before the horse. Wilson's tactlessness was, of course, a factor in the situation, and it gave the Republican reactionaries a wonderful opening. But his attitude was the excuse for rejection rather than the cause of it. Don't you think I am right?

Dr. Abraham Flexner to R. B. F.

New York   October 13, 1920

". . . . The Senate with all its factiousness was ready to

ratify the treaty and adopt the League with reservations. Had Wilson said the word, the Democrats would have voted with the Lodge people and the thing would have gone through. It was Wilson who rejected the thing with reservations, and not the Senate. Now Wilson is apparently with Cox, who apparently will accept any kind of reservation to get the thing through. Meanwhile, is it a League? France and Belgium decline to comply with one of its most important stipulations, namely, to submit to the League treaties made by members of it. The Republicans have been largely factious, but in some cases sincere. There is also in the country a large body of sincere, independent persons, feeling skeptical about the League in general and opposed to certain features of it. Wilson makes no distinction between the latter class and the factious Republicans. I can't help thinking that on his shoulders rests the real blame.

However, I would rather talk with you and fight with you than write to you.

R. B. F. to Dr. Abraham Flexner

New York   October 15, 1920

I really must come down to 61 Broadway and convert you, because you are too good a fellow to go wrong the way you are doing now. However, I cannot resist saying as follows:

1. France and Belgium did not decline to file with the Secretariat the terms of their new treaty. That is a tale you must have read in the *New York Tribune* or the *New York Herald*.

2. President Wilson made mistakes of tact and judgment *in trying to put a good plan through*.

3. The Senate seized upon these mistakes as an excuse for *not* putting the plan through.

4. Wilson's failure to make a distinction between factious Republicans and honest skeptics has nothing to do with the merits of the League of Nations.

5. Wilson's temperament, judgment, failures, second

marriage, blindness, shortsightedness, autocracy, etc., are absolutely irrelevant to the issue which confronts us, i.e., is the League of Nations a good machine to stop war? If the answer is in the negative, have you something better to suggest?

R. B. F. to the *New York Times*

New York   October 17, 1920

WILL THE LEAGUE STOP WARS?

One of the agonizing recollections of July, 1914, is the way in which the issue of peace and war rocked dizzily on the edge of the precipice. For nearly a week the situation teetered first one way and then the other, while the world in a stupor of suspense watched the frantic efforts of Sir Edward Grey to find some foothold, some leverage, by which the impending catastrophe could be averted. It seemed as if the push of a single arm or even a breath could rock the situation back to safety. And then suddenly, while Sir Edward Grey and his associates fought for an opening, the whole situation crashed to the bottom.

What had happened? The world had failed to create any machinery for the settlement of international disputes. Except for the institution at The Hague, which was a skeleton without power, there was no judicial court or arbitral body, and no obligation to resort to either before running to arms. There were no precedents to serve as guides in the peaceful adjustment of quarrels, and the pyramiding of armaments between rival nations had reached dizzy heights. When war loomed on the horizon, therefore, there was nothing to stop it. It came into being almost in a vacuum. No meeting ground was available; no obligation for delay and discussion existed. The world had gotten itself into a blind alley from which there appeared to be no escape. The catastrophe began without a single conference. A handful of hasty, misunderstood telegrams plunged the world over the brink, and the result was the greatest tragedy in human history.

The League of Nations is the world's answer to the insistent question of 7,000,000 dead who lie on Europe's battlefields. It represents an attempt to build into international relationships and to make compulsory all the factors that were lacking in 1914; delay, discussion, arbitration, law; in other words, an obligation, written into the bond, for the human family to think before it acts, and to try the processes of peace before it resorts to those of war. Sir Edward Grey knows. Let him speak of these new arrangements.

"If the machinery of the League of Nations had been in existence," he says, "indeed, if we had had any one of the half dozen avenues of escape which the Covenant provides, the tragedy of 1914 could have been averted."

R. B. F. to Dr. Abraham Flexner

New York   December 2, 1920

You are perfectly hopeless. Here you sit outside the League refusing to go in, refusing to lend your influence to help in the fight between liberalism and Toryism, and yet cussing your head off because the Tories seem to be getting the upper hand. It is just as if Washington had sulked in his tent and cussed the Continentals because the British were licking them. Get in and help! Do something about it! Grab a gun, but don't just stay outside and cuss.

In thus exhorting you, I am exhorting through you the whole of recalcitrant America.

Dr. Abraham Flexner to R. B. F.

New York   December 4, 1920

Of course I want to go into the League, but I want to have my hands in my pockets and my coat buttoned up and I want to get rid of all this sentimental talk and to realize that I am not dealing with people who are neither honest nor sincere about it. Get your friend, Harding, to appoint me as the American representative and I'll show you!

Mr. Lansing Writes a Brief

(Written for the *New York Evening Post*, March 24, 1921)

"THE PEACE NEGOTIATIONS."

By Robert Lansing. Houghton Mifflin Co.

Reviewed by RAYMOND B. FOSDICK

MR. LANSING'S book, "The Peace Negotiations," has been eagerly awaited. It has promised to be the first authentic story by a prominent participant of what happened behind the scenes in Paris. Coming from a man of Mr. Lansing's experience and training we were justified in expecting a constructive emphasis, a positive grasp of the great problems that tested the statesmanship of 1919, and above all a breadth of vision and an intolerance of petty things which would lift the whole business out of the realm of personal quarrels and misunderstandings.

But alas for human expectations! Mr. Lansing is concerned only with himself and his relations with the President. He does not even pretend to write a book about the Peace Conference, and the title that he has chosen is utterly misleading. It should have been called: "My Difficulties With Woodrow Wilson." "The time has come for a frank account of our differences," he says, and he proceeds to list seven of them which form the basis of his discussion. In other words, the book is merely a brief in his own defence, an elaborated catalogue of misunderstandings, "a refutation of Mr. Wilson's implied charge that I was not loyal to him as President." With the world face to face with the question whether civilization itself has not been brought to its doom through the war and the Treaty of Versailles, Mr. Lansing, as one of the chief actors in the tragedy, sits himself down to answer this question: "In forming an opinion as to my differences with the President it should be the reader's endeavor to place himself in my position at the time and not judge them solely by the results of the negotiations at Paris. It comes down to this: Was I justified then? Am I justified now?"

One is tempted to shriek: "In the name of God, what does it matter and who cares?"

R. B. F. to the *New York Times*

New York   August 4, 1921

The attitude of our State Department in refusing to answer official communications from the League of Nations may be explained as a deliberate effort to hasten the dissolution of that organization. But on the face of the reports from Washington it is something more serious. It is, in fact, an individual slight to each of the forty-eight nations that have accepted the plan of international cooperation repudiated by our own Senate.

The department seems to take the position that the League is a body wholly separate from the Governments belonging to it and that it is trying to intrude itself between those Governments and the United States. This intrusion is virtuously resented by the United States, not only on its own behalf but on behalf of the other Governments involved. It would be hard to conceive a more erroneous idea of the relationship between the League and the Governments back of it. The League not only is a creation of the forty-eight Governments belonging to it, but it is a part of all those Governments. It has no existence except through them and on their behalf. What it implies is that those forty-eight Governments have pooled certain interests and certain activities for greater efficiency, believing that by acting cooperatively they can save time, money, and friction. With this purpose in view, they have established the League and made it an extension, so to speak, of their respective foreign departments.

League of Nations

Editorial from the *New York Tribune*

New York   August 5, 1921

COLLECTIVE INSULTS

That the unwillingness of the State Department to deal directly with the League of Nations constitutes the "equivalent to an attempt on the part of the government to interfere with the rights of all the forty-eight governments belonging to the League to organize their own affairs in any manner which may be deemed most effective to themselves" is the extraordinary conclusion of Mr. Raymond B. Fosdick in a letter addressed to The *Times.*

This is indeed a strange method of reasoning. The League, says Mr. Fosdick, is not only a creation of the forty-eight governments belonging to it, but it is a part of all these governments, and hence an insult to the League is an insult to all its members individually. The League is a collective body, an entity by itself, for purposes of functioning, but relating to matters of insult is a porcupine with forty-eight quills. "Love me, love all my dogs," is its attitude.

This is deplorable. Think of our State Department deliberately insulting forty-eight nations each time the League sends in a communication and gets no answer. This means that for the last ten communications Mr. Hughes has returned 480 insults. Can it be that these nations have all learned to turn the other cheek or—worse still—do not exactly reason as does Mr. Fosdick?

Editorial from the *New York Tribune*

New York   September 22, 1921

THE BLUE WILSONITES

Bad faith, bad judgment, political skulduggery and a callous sacrifice of the peace of the world to satisfy political exigencies are some of the charges made by Raymond B. Fosdick against the Harding Administration's development of

133

the plan for the Conference on the Limitation of Armament. . . .

Mr. Harding, Mr. Fosdick says, has made success impossible because he has not invited the Hejaz, Abyssinia and Ethiopia to send delegates. "Is there not danger," Mr. Fosdick darkly asks, "that the discriminatory basis of the conference may wreck beyond repair the possibility of world disarmament?" . . . .

But these are mere incidents. The worst error of all is the continued refusal to accept the present League and all its work forthwith. The Administration "has even gone to the extreme of sending a local consular officer to the League Secretariat with a verbal explanation that the United States, not being a member of the League, could not answer its communications."

Mr. Fosdick is, of course, a most excellent gentleman. Hence the greater pity that he cannot recover from the results of the election. When Henry Clay was defeated the last time a large number of Silver Gray Whigs took to their beds. What may be called the Blue Wilsonites fall on the floor and only rave.

R. B. F. to the *New York Tribune*

New York   September 25, 1921

If, to be a "Blue Wilsonite," as charged in your editorial of Thursday, is to believe that the United States ought to enter the League of Nations, I suppose I might as well plead guilty. But your further comment on my ability to "recover from the result of the election" requires a rejoinder.

What, may I ask, was the result of the election as far as the League of Nations was concerned? I seem to recall an earnest appeal signed by such men as Mr. Hughes, Mr. Hoover, Mr. Wickersham, Mr. Root, Mr. Taft, Mr. Stimson and twenty-five other eminent Republican leaders, pleading with the American people for votes for Mr. Harding on the ground that the Republican party and its candidate were "bound by every consideration of good faith" to have the United States enter the existing League of Nations, with such modifications as necessity might require. Was this statement merely a political maneuver to get votes? Did the result of the election mean that the United States was not to enter the League of Nations? If the answer is in the negative, then why are those who advocate the carrying out of this pre-election policy of the Republicans consigned to outer darkness?

When the *Tribune* is able to report to its readers that this pledge of the Republican leaders has been redeemed and is no longer a scrap of paper, the "Blue Wilsonites" will immediately recover from their mania.

Editorial from the *Great Falls* (Montana) *Leader*[1]

Great Falls   September 30, 1921

. . . . It will be remembered that Raymond Fosdick is the man appointed by former President Wilson as America's representative on the Secretariat of the league of nations. To be sure the league was not then, and never has been, approved by the United States, but Mr. Wilson anticipated a victory for his precious covenant by selecting some of the patronage thereunder. When Fosdick sailed for Europe he had visions of a long and pleasant life on the shores of Lake Geneva, supported in luxury by a princely salary from the league exchequer. But the dream was rudely shattered when the Versailles treaty was rejected, and Raymond found himself out of a job. Naturally his attitude toward the party that accomplished the league's downfall is not the most charitable. . . . Fortunately, there are not many Fosdicks in the United States today.

R. B. F. to the *Chicago Tribune*

New York   December 4, 1921

I am amazed at your charge of extravagance against the League of Nations. The $140,000,000 which Congress has

[1] This editorial was syndicated in a large number of western papers. It was first published by the National Republican Committee.

just voted for ten new cruisers in the navy would run the Court of International Justice for 368 years, and would cover the entire cost of the League, including the Court, for twenty-nine years—long after the cruisers had been given to the junkman.

Dr. Abraham Flexner to R. B. F.

New York   February 26, 1922

. . . . Don't believe for a moment that my feeling about international relations springs from any belief that we are in virtue superior to the people over there. I know perfectly well that we are not. In many important respects we may even be inferior; but that does not seem to me to be the determining consideration when it comes to international action upon all questions. The thing that influences my opinion is this—we are historically and geographically fortunate in being able to throw most of our attention and effort into our domestic concerns. Our problems and inter-ests are mainly, of course not wholly, domestic. On the Continent, geography, history, habit minimize domestic, that is, social problems, and enormously emphasize exter-nal relations. . . . My unwillingness to pledge ourselves to sit in at all European conferences is due therefore to a feeling that it would involve us in an unequal game in the course of which we should lose, not gain, in actual influence. Had we been in the League of Nations, there could never have been a Washington conference. The Genoa thing is, as far as I can make out, something that we ought not to enter until we see the kind of thing it is likely to be.

I am infinitely sorry for all Europe. It is struggling under a burden too heavy to be borne; but, taking our people as they are and our position as it is, I can't help thinking that in the long run we shall be able to help most if we keep out, throwing our weight into the scale from time to time when-ever a specific good can be accomplished thereby.

As far as the League is concerned, it might as well be in

Mars. The Silesian decision killed it.[1] How much better it would have been, had the League decided that question righteously and soundly, and died in consequence thereof! In that event it would have at any rate had an honorable end and people would have believed that it was possible to constitute an international tribunal which had the courage of its own ideals. As it is, the League is just another name for ordinary European diplomacy and as such has, as far as I can make out, already lost all moral authority. However, time will tell. . . .

R. B. F. to Dr. Abraham Flexner

New York   March 17, 1922

. . . . Don't you think you are attempting to build too soundproof a partition between international relations and domestic concerns? In your letter you say that America is fortunately able to give most of its attention to domestic interests, while on the continent history and habit enormously emphasize external relations, although in England the best minds are concerned about internal problems precisely as we here in the United States are. I wish it were possible for each nation to banish the nightmare of international relations once and for all. I wish we could live as we used to live one hundred years ago in blissful isolation. But those days are past and the world is bound together in so intimate a way now that there is scarcely an internal problem that does not have international reverberations. Here in the

[1] The Treaty of Versailles decided that the people of Upper Silesia should determine by plebiscite whether they belonged to Germany or Poland. The plebiscite proved inconclusive, and the Allied and Associated Powers finally agreed to leave the decision to a commission of the Council of the League of Nations. The Council, in turn, recommended that an advisory "Upper Silesian Mixed Commission" should be set up for a period of fifteen years, together with an arbitral tribunal for settling private disputes occasioned by the temporary measures. On the whole, the industrial provisions suggested by the League worked unexpectedly smoothly, but the question was always a thorny one, and caused, on occasion, a great deal of bitterness.

United States our domestic problems are all shot to pieces, due to our upset international situation. We are faced with gigantic problems right at our own door-sills which we cannot solve until we solve the question of our relations with our neighbors in Europe. The two sets of problems cannot be divorced. The Atlantic Ocean is no longer the barrier it used to be. You say that industrially and economically England is hitched to the continent. In the same way we are hitched there too—whether we like it or not. The picture that you draw of Lloyd George with one foot in France and the other in Downing Street is painful, but that is going to be the necessary posture of our statesmen in the future until we can get some kind of international machinery that will give us enough assurance of peace to allow us to attend to our domestic concerns.

It would be much easier to argue this out with you over a luncheon table, and I wish I could be with you this minute. I should like to tell you something about that Upper Silesian decision that you refer to. I don't think that it has killed the League for one minute. . . .

John Randolph Bolling[1] to R. B. F.

Washington   March 21, 1922

It is very generous of you to offer to undertake the inquiries which Mr. Wilson receives regarding the League of Nations.

Enclosed is one which came to him this morning. In the future I will simply send them along to you, and of course it will not be necessary to make any acknowledgment of the receipt.

Please don't go to too much trouble in the matter, or I will feel that I am imposing on you. In the majority of instances the inquirers seem to want simply printed matter.

[1] Secretary to Woodrow Wilson after he left the White House and was living on S Street in Washington.

League of Nations

R. B. F. to Woodrow Wilson

New York April 25, 1922

I am sending you herewith a summary of the work of the League of Nations during its first two years, published by the Information Section of the Secretariat. It is possible that you have already seen it, but as it came to me from Geneva only the other day, I am venturing to forward the copy to you.

I know that it must be with keen satisfaction that you are watching the growing prestige and authority of the League. It is steadily winning for itself a place from which it can never be dislodged, and is establishing itself as the only possible agency for maintaining the world's peace. To it the nations will inevitably turn for an answer to their difficulties when the hopes of the Washington and Genoa Conferences have turned to ashes, and all the other substitutes have failed.

I think of you in these hours of vindication with an increasing affection. The point of view which you gave us in the classroom at Princeton I have never forgotten, and I know with what a serene and smiling faith you are facing the future, confident of the foundations of your work and of its lasting place in the life of men. God is on our side in this business and the future is secure.

Woodrow Wilson to R. B. F.

Washington April 27, 1922

Thank you for sending me the summary of the League's work for the first two years. I shall examine it with the greatest interest. The League has indeed become a vital and commanding force and will more and more dominate international relationships. I am thankful that I had something to do with its institution and I am also thankful, my dear fellow, that it has drawn to its service men like yourself in whose ideals and purposes I have perfect confidence.

I hope that the future will afford us many opportunities of counsel and cooperation.

R. B. F. to Dr. Abraham Flexner

New York   February 4, 1924

.... You say that Wilson failed in the greatest opportunity that has in our lifetime, come to any man. I cannot agree with this—unless you and I have different definitions of failure. If to see one's ideals succeed in one's own lifetime is "success," then I admit that Wilson failed, but on this basis history would record a long list of "failures"—Socrates, the second Isaiah, Jesus, Savonarola, Galileo, not to mention a score of others.

My point is not necessarily that Wilson should be included in this list of the immortals. We are too near him to know what his place in history is going to be. But to say that he "failed" seems to me to be a squint-eyed way of looking at history. In other words, I don't believe you can appraise the success or failure of a spiritual ideal within the measure of a man's lifetime....

Dr. Abraham Flexner to R. B. F.

New York   February 5, 1924

It was very nice indeed of you, busy as you are, to write me about Wilson.

I had read your eulogy and I thought, as a eulogy, it was excellent, but it was still a eulogy—not an effort at historic appreciation. Let me explain what I mean by the word, "failure," and why no matter what happens in the future, I think the word, failure, will have to be used in describing his connection with the League. The men with whom you compare him were prophets and scientists. I note that you call Wilson a "prophet," but, my dear boy, he was not a prophet. He was President of the United States and as such had a concern for policies which neither Socrates nor Jesus nor Galileo had. He did more to get us *in* and more to keep us *out* of the League than any other man, and I call him as a statesman a failure, because through self-will, inflexibility, egotism, failure to distinguish between the essential and inessential, he successfully defeated *his own* and the country's *purpose*. Suppose Abraham Lincoln or Dr. Buttrick had been president, would they not have listened to Hymans[1] and Lord Grey—they wouldn't have needed Hymans or Lord Grey—to tell them to concede every minor point, in order to compass the one important one, namely accession to the League? A statesman would have called Lodge and Reed to the White House, would have furnished them pads and reams of white paper, would have told them to write every reservation that they could imagine and would thus have disarmed them and probably have reduced both the number and importance of the reservations. But whether it would have worked this way or would have resulted in reams of reservations, we would have been in the League and the whole history of the last six years and the next one hundred would have been different. If we ultimately join, Wilson will have succeeded as a prophet. He would still have failed as a statesman.

Wherein is this analysis faulty?

R. B. F. to Dr. Abraham Flexner

New York   February 6, 1924

No, I think you are wrong. It seems to me you are confusing the work of Wilson as a prophet and teacher on the one hand, and, on the other, the particular technique through which he attempted to put his ideas into effect. His technique was often faulty, but the ideals he stood for represent, to my way of thinking, a new hope for the future. He stood at a cross-road in history and pointed out a new path. What you are objecting to is the method he used in pointing. You say that his tactics in getting the race to follow on the

[1] Paul Hymans was a Belgian statesman who represented Belgium at the Treaty of Versailles.

new path were wrong. I grant you that they were not always right, but I come back to this: that he *pointed the way*.

If you are going to insist that all the prophets in history shall be eminent strategists, you are going to have very few men whom you can call great. Confucius made some shocking mistakes in tactics; Socrates was constantly and needlessly antagonistic; Isaiah, as far as we know, made quite a mess of his life, and Galileo recanted on everything that he had stood for. When you can combine great ideals with good tactics you have an extraordinary combination; but good tactics is the lesser part. To rule a man out because while he has the former he has not the latter is to lose the essence of the matter.

R. B. F. to the *New York World*

New York   February 24, 1924

WOODROW WILSON AND THE LEAGUE OF NATIONS[1]

. . . . Whatever we may think at this moment of the career of Woodrow Wilson, on this point we can be well agreed: that he laid down his life for an ideal. And what *was* that ideal? It was that the secret to the peace of the world could be found if only the creative intelligence of mankind could be harnessed to the task. That is, he believed that peace was not a matter of hopes or pious wishes. It must be definitely planned for. Just as we set up machinery of arbitration and conciliation in advance of labor difficulties to meet the situations as they arise, so in the field of international relations there must be concrete methods in existence to absorb the shock and lessen the friction of the contacts between nations.

Constantly in Woodrow Wilson's mind was the memory of July, 1914. Do you remember those days? It seemed almost inconceivable that war could come. Here in the United States we watched with breathless interest the efforts of Sir

[1] Woodrow Wilson died February 3, 1924.

Edward Grey as he tried to get a foothold in that situation. But it was too late. There were no precedents. There was no machinery and in that pitch of flame and heat the necessary machinery could not be extemporized. The war began without a single conference—without a single meeting around a table. A handful of hasty, misunderstood telegrams plunged the world over the brink into the greatest catastrophe ever visited upon the human race.

That was the background out of which the League of Nations was born. "It never must happen again," Mr. Wilson said. And so he wove into the treaties of peace a plan for the future, in the hope that thereby succeeding generations might be spared the cataclysm that had overtaken his own—and for that plan he laid down his life.

The League of Nations is now four years old. It comprises 54 nations—seven-eighths of the civilized world. It includes all of Europe except Germany and Russia; all of North and South America except the United States, Mexico and Ecuador; all of Asia except Afghanistan; and all Africa. The Allied Supreme Council, which was the most powerful military alliance the world has ever known, and the "Association of Nations" vaguely proposed in America, are now mere history, leaving the League alone in the field of international organization. . . .

This was Woodrow Wilson's vision and this was the ideal for which he laid down his life. Two weeks before he died I talked with him at his home in Washington. His whole thought was of the League of Nations and its promise for the future. In vivid, burning words he spoke of the day when the authority of law would be substituted for the authority of force. This was America's opportunity. This was America's contribution to the world. This was our chance to add immeasurably to the spiritual resources of the race. In his earnestness the tears rolled down his face, and when I pledged him on behalf of the younger generation that we would carry through to a finish the thing that he had started, he gave way completely. My last impression of him was of a grim, determined jaw, a tear-stained face, and a faint voice whispering "God bless you." With his white hair, and gray, lined face he seemed like the reincarnation of Isaiah crying to his country: "Awake, Awake, Oh Zion. Put on thy beautiful garments, Oh Jerusalem." "Oh Jerusalem, Thou that stonest the prophets!"

R. B. F. to his Family

London   July 19, 1919

I conclude this small volume with a letter out of chronological order. By rights it should have been near the beginning, between my questioning letter to Walter Lippmann and his reply. But it expresses, perhaps better than any other, my inmost feelings about the League of Nations, and they were feelings that stayed with me through the period covered by this volume and in later years when I continued to campaign for American participation in the League.

This letter was written during the gloomy period when the great victory parade was staged in London. Americans, French, Italians, Czechoslovaks, Japanese, Chinese, Portuguese, and thousands of Britain's own troops marched in the seven-mile route which ended when the King took the salute in front of Buckingham Palace. "It was a thrilling and deeply moving spectacle." I wrote my family, "and yet in a sense terribly depressing."

The American troops came first, headed by Pershing on a spirited horse which danced all over the street; but Pershing is a superb horseman and it was obvious that he was enjoying himself. Our troops were truly magnificent. They evidently had been carefully picked and drilled. They were all six footers, and in new uniforms and freshly varnished helmets they marched past with the snap and precision of West Point cadets. . . .

Foch headed the French troops, riding on a quiet, little horse. He looked neither to the right nor to the left.

French soldiers always seem to me to be indifferent march-
ers, but today in their battle-worn uniforms and with
their long, menacing bayonets they looked like the tough,
gallant soldiers they are.

But it was the British troops that really swept the crowd
off its feet in an emotion such as I have never seen. The
hundreds of thousands of people who were packed along
the curbs wept more than they cheered. Everybody was in
tears. Particularly when the broken ranks of the Old
Contemptibles swept by—the men who fought at Mons
and the First Battle of the Marne—a sob broke from the
crowd that you could hear way up the street.

They called it a Victory parade, but it was the saddest
thing I have ever seen, because it was really a funeral
march for 5,000,000 Allied soldiers who are buried on the
Continent. I don't suppose there will ever be a sight like
that again . . . .

At the end we walked back to Sunderland House in a
pretty grim and sober mood. So much depends on the
League of Nations. The obstacles in the way are really
frightening, but somehow or other it has got to be made
to work . . . .

COVENANT OF THE LEAGUE OF NATIONS

Adopted at the Plenary Session
of the
Interallied Peace Conference
April 28, 1919

The High Contracting Parties in order to promote international cooperation and to achieve international peace and security by the acceptance of obligations not to resort to war, by the prescription of open, just and honorable relations between nations, by the firm establishment of the understandings of international law as the actual rule of conduct among Governments, and by the maintenance of justice and a scrupulous respect for all treaty obligations in the dealings of organized peoples with one another, agree to this Covenant of the League of Nations:

ARTICLE I

1. The original members of the League of Nations shall be those of the signatories which are named in the annex to this Covenant and also such of those other states named in the annex as shall accede without reservation to this Covenant. Such accessions shall be effected by a declaration deposited with the Secretariat within two months of the coming into force of the Covenant. Notice thereof shall be sent to all other members of the League.

2. Any fully self-governing state, dominion or colony not named in the annex may become a member of the League if its admission is agreed to by two-thirds of the Assembly, provided that it shall give effective guaranties of its sincere intention to observe its international obligations, and shall accept such regulations as may be prescribed by the League in regard to its military and naval forces and armaments.

3. Any member of the League may, after two years' notice of its intention so to do, withdraw from the League, provided that all its international obligations and all its obligations under this Covenant shall have been fulfilled at the time of its withdrawal.

ARTICLE II

1. The action of the League under this Covenant shall be effected through the instrumentality of an Assembly and of a Council, with a permanent Secretariat.

147

ARTICLE III

1. The Assembly shall consist of representatives of the members of the League.

2. The Assembly shall meet at stated intervals and from time to time as occasion may require at the seat of the League, or at such other place as may be decided upon.

3. The Assembly may deal at its meetings with any matter within the sphere of action of the League or affecting the peace of the world.

4. At meetings of the Assembly each member of the League shall have one vote, and may have not more than three representatives.

ARTICLE IV

1. The Council shall consist of representatives of the United States of America, of the British Empire, of France, of Italy, and of Japan, together with representatives of four other members of the League. These four members of the League shall be selected by the Assembly from time to time in its discretion. Until the appointment of the representatives of the four members of the League first selected by the Assembly, representatives of Belgium, Brazil, Greece and Spain shall be members of the Council.

2. With the approval of the majority of the Assembly, the Council may name additional members of the League whose representatives shall always be members of the Council; the Council with like approval may increase the number of members of the League to be selected by the Assembly for representation on the Council.

3. The Council shall meet from time to time as occasion may require, and at least once a year, at the seat of the League, or at such other place as may be decided upon.

4. The Council may deal at its meetings with any matter within the sphere of action of the League or affecting the peace of the world.

5. Any member of the League not represented on the Council shall be invited to send a representative to sit as a member at any meeting of the Council during the consideration of matters specially affecting the interests of that member of the League.

6. At meetings of the Council each member of the League represented on the Council shall have one vote, and may have not more than one representative.

ARTICLE V

1. Except where otherwise expressly provided in this Covenant, or by the terms of this treaty, decisions at any meeting of the Assembly or of the Council shall require the agreement of all the members of the League represented at the meeting.

2. All matters of procedure at meetings of the Assembly or of the Council, including the appointment of committees to investigate particular matters, shall be regulated by the Assembly or by the Council and may be decided by a majority of the members of the League represented at the meeting.

3. The first meeting of the Assembly and the first meeting of the Council shall be summoned by the President of the United States of America.

ARTICLE VI

1. The permanent Secretariat shall be established at the seat of the League. The Secretariat shall comprise a Secretary-General and such secretaries and staff as may be required.

2. The first Secretary-General shall be the person named in the annex; thereafter the Secretary-General shall be appointed by the Council with the approval of the majority of the Assembly.

3. The secretaries and the staff of the Secretariat shall be appointed by the Secretary-General with the approval of the Council.

4. The Secretary-General shall act in that capacity at all meetings of the Assembly and of the Council.

5. The expenses of the Secretariat shall be borne by the members of the League in accordance with the apportionment of the expenses of the International Bureau of the Universal Postal Union.

ARTICLE VII

1. The seat of the League is established at Geneva.

2. The Council may at any time decide that the seat of the League shall be established elsewhere.

3. All positions under or in connection with the League, including the Secretariat, shall be open equally to men and women.

4. Representatives of the members of the League and officials of the League when engaged on the business of the League shall enjoy diplomatic privileges and immunities.

5. The buildings and other property occupied by the League or its officials or by representatives attending its meetings shall be inviolable.

ARTICLE VIII

1. The members of the League recognize that the maintenance of peace requires the reduction of national armaments to the lowest point consistent with national safety and the enforcement by common action of international obligations.

2. The Council, taking account of the geographical situation and circumstances of each member, shall formulate plans for such reduction for the consideration and action of the several Governments.

3. Such plans shall be subject to reconsideration and revision at least every 10 years.

4. After these plans shall have been adopted by the several Governments, the limits of armaments therein fixed shall not be exceeded without the concurrence of the Council.

5. The members of the League agree that the manufacture by private enterprise of munitions and implements of war is open to grave objections. The Council shall advise how the evil effects attendant upon such manufacture can be prevented, due regard being had to the necessities of those members of the League which are not able to manufacture the munitions and implements of war necessary for their safety.

6. The members of the League undertake to interchange full and frank information as to the scale of their armaments, their military and naval programs, and the condition of such of their industries as are adaptable to warlike purposes.

ARTICLE IX

1. A permanent commission shall be constituted to advise the Council on the execution of the provisions of Articles I and VIII and on military and naval questions generally.

ARTICLE X

1. The members of the League undertake to respect and preserve as against external aggression the territorial integrity and existing political independence of all members of the League. In case of any such aggression or in case of any threat or danger of such aggression, the Council shall advise upon the means by which this obligation shall be fulfilled.

ARTICLE XI

1. Any war or threat of war, whether immediately affecting any of the members of the League or not, is hereby declared a matter

of concern to the whole League, and the League shall take any action that may be deemed wise and effectual to safeguard the peace of nations. In case any such emergency should arise, the Secretary-General shall, on the request of any member of the League, forthwith summon a meeting of the Council.

2. It is also declared to be the friendly right of each member of the League to bring to the attention of the Assembly or of the Council any circumstance whatever affecting international relations which threatens to disturb either the peace or the good understanding between nations upon which peace depends.

ARTICLE XII

1. The members of the League agree that, if there should arise between them any dispute likely to lead to a rupture, they will submit the matter either to arbitration or to inquiry by the Council, and they agree in no case to resort to war until three months after the award by the arbitrators or the report by the Council.

2. In any case under this article the award of the arbitrators shall be made within a reasonable time, and the report of the Council shall be made within six months after the submission of the dispute.

ARTICLE XIII

1. The members of the League agree that, whenever any dispute shall arise between them which they recognize to be suitable for submission to arbitration and which cannot be satisfactorily settled by diplomacy, they will submit the whole subject matter to arbitration.

2. Disputes as to the interpretation of a treaty, as to any question of international law, as to the existence of any fact which if established would constitute a breach of any international obligation, or as to the extent and nature of the reparation to be made for any such breach, are declared to be among those which are generally suitable for submission to arbitration.

3. For the consideration of any such dispute the court of arbitration to which the case is referred shall be the court agreed on by the parties to the dispute or stipulated in any convention existing between them.

4. The members of the League agree that they will carry out in full good faith any award that may be rendered and that they will not resort to war against a member of the League which complies therewith. In the event of any failure to carry out such

an award, the Council shall propose what steps should be taken to give effect thereto.

ARTICLE XIV

1. The Council shall formulate and submit to the members of the League for adoption plans for the establishment of a permanent Court of International Justice. The Court shall be competent to hear and determine any dispute of an international character which the parties thereto submit to it. The court may also give an advisory opinion upon any dispute or question referred to it by the Council or by the Assembly.

ARTICLE XV

1. If there should arise between members of the League any dispute likely to lead to a rupture, which is not submitted to arbitration as above, the members of the League agree that they will submit the matter to the Council. Any party to the dispute may effect such submission by giving notice of the existence of the dispute to the Secretary-General, who will make all necessary arrangements for a full investigation and consideration thereof.

2. For this purpose the parties to the dispute will communicate to the Secretary-General, as promptly as possible, statements of their case, with all the relevant facts and papers, and the Council may forthwith direct the publication thereof.

3. The Council shall endeavor to effect a settlement of the dispute and, if such efforts are successful, a statement shall be made public giving such facts and explanations regarding the dispute and terms of settlement thereof as the Council may deem appropriate.

4. If the dispute is not thus settled, the Council either unanimously or by a majority vote shall make and publish a report containing a statement of the facts of the dispute and the recommendations which are deemed just and proper in regard thereto.

5. Any member of the League represented on the Council may make public a statement of the facts of the dispute and of its conclusions regarding the same.

6. If a report by the Council is unanimously agreed to by the members thereof other than the representatives of one or more of the parties to the dispute, the members of the League agree that they will not go to war with any party to the dispute which complies with the recommendations of the report.

7. If the Council fails to reach a report which is unanimously agreed to by the members thereof, other than the representatives

of one or more of the parties to the dispute, the members of the League reserve to themselves the right to take such action as they shall consider necessary for the maintenance of right and justice.

8. If the dispute between the parties is claimed by one of them, and is found by the Council, to arise out of a matter which by international law is solely within the domestic jurisdiction of that party, the Council shall so report and shall make no recommendation as to its settlement.

9. The Council may in any case under this article refer the dispute to the Assembly. The dispute shall be so referred at the request of either party to the dispute, provided that such request be made within 14 days after the submission of the dispute to the Council.

10. In any case referred to the Assembly, all the provisions of this article and of Article XII relating to the action and powers of the Council shall apply to the action and powers of the Assembly, provided that a report made by the Assembly, if concurred in by the representatives of those members of the League represented on the Council and of a majority of the other members of the League, exclusive in each case of the representatives of the parties to the dispute, shall have the same force as a report by the Council concurred in by all the members thereof other than the representatives of one or more of the parties to the dispute.

ARTICLE XVI

1. Should any member of the League resort to war in disregard of its covenants under Articles XII, XIII or XV, it shall *ipso facto* be deemed to have committed an act of war against all other members of the League, which hereby undertake immediately to subject it to the severance of all trade or financial relations, the prohibition of all intercourse between their nationals and the nationals of the covenant-breaking member of the League, and the prevention of all financial, commercial or personal intercourse between the nationals of the covenant-breaking member of the League and the nationals of any other state, whether a member of the League or not.

2. It shall be the duty of the Council in such case to recommend to the several Governments concerned what effective military or naval force the members of the League shall severally contribute to the armed forces to be used to protect the covenants of the League.

3. The members of the League agree, further, that they will

mutually support one another in the financial and economic measures which are taken under this article, in order to minimize the loss and inconvenience resulting from the above measures, and that they will mutually support one another in resisting any special measures aimed at one of their number by the covenant-breaking member of the League, and that they will take the necessary steps to afford passage through their territory to the forces of any of the members of the League which are co-operating to protect the covenants of the League.

4. Any member of the League which has violated any covenant of the League may be declared to be no longer a member of the League by a vote of the Council concurred in by the representatives of all the other members of the League represented thereon.

ARTICLE XVII

1. In the event of a dispute between a member of the League and a state which is not a member of the League, or between states not members of the League, the state or states not members of the League shall be invited to accept the obligations of membership in the League for the purposes of such dispute, upon such conditions as the Council may deem just. If such invitation is accepted, the provisions of Articles XII to XVI, inclusive, shall be applied with such modifications as may be deemed necessary by the Council.

2. Upon such invitation being given, the Council shall immediately institute an inquiry into the circumstances of the dispute and recommend such action as may seem best and most effectual in the circumstances.

3. If a state so invited shall refuse to accept the obligations of membership in the League for the purposes of such dispute, and shall resort to war against a member of the League, the provisions of Article XVI shall be applicable as against the state taking such action.

4. If both parties to the dispute, when so invited, refuse to accept the obligations of membership in the League for the purposes of such dispute, the Council may take such measures and make such recommendations as will prevent hostilities and will result in the settlement of the dispute.

ARTICLE XVIII

1. Every treaty or international engagement entered into henceforward by any member of the League shall be forthwith

registered with the Secretariat and shall as soon as possible be published by it. No such treaty or international engagement shall be binding until so registered.

ARTICLE XIX

1. The Assembly may from time to time advise the reconsideration by members of the League of treaties which have become inapplicable, and the consideration of international conditions whose continuance might endanger the peace of the world.

ARTICLE XX

1. The members of the League severally agree that this Covenant is accepted as abrogating all obligations or understandings *inter se* which are inconsistent with the terms thereof, and solemnly undertake that they will not hereafter enter into any engagements inconsistent with the terms thereof.

2. In case any member of the League shall, before becoming a member of the League, have undertaken any obligations inconsistent with the terms of this Covenant, it shall be the duty of such member to take immediate steps to procure its release from such obligations.

ARTICLE XXI

1. Nothing in this Covenant shall be deemed to affect the validity of international engagements such as treaties of arbitration or regional understandings like the Monroe doctrine for securing the maintenance of peace.

ARTICLE XXII

1. To those colonies and territories which as a consequence of the late war have ceased to be under the sovereignty of the states which formerly governed them and which are inhabited by peoples not yet able to stand by themselves under the strenuous conditions of the modern world, there should be applied the principle that the well being and development of such peoples form a sacred trust of civilization and that securities for the performance of this trust should be embodied in this Covenant.

2. The best method of giving practical effect to this principle is that the tutelage of such peoples should be intrusted to advanced nations who, by reason of their resources, their experience or their geographical position, can best undertake this responsibility and who are willing to accept it, and that this tutelage should be exercised by them as mandatories on behalf of the League.

155

3. The character of the mandate must differ according to the stage of the development of the people, the geographical situation of the territory, its economic conditions, and other similar circumstances.

4. Certain communities formerly belonging to the Turkish Empire have reached a stage of development where their existence as independent nations can be provisionally recognized subject to the rendering of administrative advice and assistance by a mandatory until such time as they are able to stand alone. The wishes of these communities must be a principal consideration in the selection of the mandatory.

5. Other peoples, especially those of Central Africa, are at such a stage that the mandatory must be responsible for the administration of the territory under conditions which will guarantee freedom of conscience and religion, subject only to the maintenance of public order and morals, the prohibition of abuses such as the slave trade, the arms traffic and the liquor traffic, and the prevention of the establishment of fortifications or military and naval bases and of military training of the natives for other than police purposes and for the defense of territory, and will also secure equal opportunities for the trade and commerce of other members of the League.

6. There are territories, such as Southwest Africa and certain of the South Pacific islands, which, owing to the sparseness of their population or their small size, or their remoteness from the centers of civilization, or their geographical contiguity to the territory of the mandatory, and other circumstances, can be best administered under the laws of the mandatory as integral portions of its territory, subject to the safeguards above mentioned in the interests of the indigenous population.

7. In every case of mandate the mandatory shall render to the Council an annual report in reference to the territory committed to its charge.

8. The degree of authority, control or administration to be exercised by the mandatory shall, if not previously agreed upon by the members of the League, be explicitly defined in each case by the Council.

9. A permanent commission shall be constituted to receive and examine the annual reports of the mandatories, and to advise the Council on all matters relating to the observance of the mandates.

ARTICLE XXIII

1. Subject to and in accordance with the provisions of international conventions existing or hereafter to be agreed upon, the members of the League:

(a) will endeavor to secure and maintain fair and humane conditions of labor for men, women and children, both in their own countries and in all countries to which their commercial and industrial relations extend, and for that purpose will establish and maintain the necessary international organizations;

(b) undertake to secure just treatment of the native inhabitants of territories under their control;

(c) will intrust the League with the general supervision over the execution of agreements with regard to the traffic in women and children and the traffic in opium and other dangerous drugs;

(d) will intrust the League with the general supervision of the trade in arms and ammunition with the countries in which the control of this traffic is necessary in the common interest;

(e) will make provision to secure and maintain freedom of communications and of transit and equitable treatment for the commerce of all members of the League. In this connection, the special necessities of the regions devastated during the war of 1914-1918 shall be borne in mind;

(f) will endeavor to take steps in matters of international concern for the prevention and control of disease.

ARTICLE XXIV

1. There shall be placed under the direction of the League all International Bureaus already established by general treaties, if the parties to such treaties consent. All such International Bureaus and all Commissions for the regulation of matters of international interest hereafter constituted shall be placed under the direction of the League.

2. In all matters of international interest which are regulated by general conventions but which are not placed under the control of international bureaus or commissions, the Secretariat of the League shall, subject to the consent of the Council and if desired by the parties, collect and distribute all relevant information and shall render any other assistance which may be necessary or desirable.

3. The Council may include as part of the expenses of the Secretariat the expenses of any Bureau or Commission which is placed under the direction of the League.

ARTICLE XXV

1. The members of the League agree to encourage and promote the establishment and co-operation of duly authorized voluntary national Red Cross organizations having as purposes the improve-

ment of health, the prevention of disease and the mitigation of suffering throughout the world.

ARTICLE XXVI

AMENDMENTS

1. Amendments to this Covenant will take effect when ratified by the members of the League whose representatives compose the Council and by a majority of the members of the League whose representatives compose the Assembly.

2. No such amendment shall bind any member of the League which signifies its dissent therefrom, but in that case it shall cease to be a member of the League.

ANNEX

I. Original members of the League of Nations, signatories of the treaty of peace:

United States of America	Cuba	Liberia
Belgium	Czecho-Slovakia	Nicaragua
Bolivia	Ecuador	Panama
Brazil	France	Peru
British Empire	Greece	Poland
Canada	Guatemala	Portugal
Australia	Haiti	Rumania
South Africa	Hedjaz	Serbia
New Zealand	Honduras	Siam
India	Italy	Uruguay
China	Japan	

States invited to accede to the Covenant:

Argentine Republic	Norway	Sweden
Chile	Paraguay	Switzerland
Colombia	Persia	Venezuela
Denmark	Salvador	
Netherlands	Spain	

II. First Secretary-General of the League of Nations: The Honorable Sir James Eric Drummond, K.C.M.G., C.B.

INDEX

Abyssinia, 134
Adriatic Sea, 50
Afghanistan, 143
Africa, 12n, 124, 143. *See also specific countries*
Allied and Associated Powers, League of Nations Council and, 11, 12, 14-15, 23, 101; League duties and, 13, 20, 21; U.S. League membership and, 52, 70, 77, 78, 79, 86; League seat and, 66, 82; World War I costs, 126, 145. *See also specific countries*
Allied Maritime Transport Council, 22
Allied Supreme Council, 36-37, 143
Alsace-Lorraine, 35
America, *see* United States of America
American colonies, 23
American Information Service, 46n
American Peace Delegation, in Paris, 18n, 46n, 59n, 99n
Ames, Mr. (League Financial Director), 92
annexations, 13
Aquitania, 5, 122
Argentine Republic, 158
armaments, 125-26, 129. *See also* disarmament
Armenia, 34
Armistice (1918), 95
Armstrong, Hamilton Fish, 63
army recruitment, conscript, 13; in mandate areas, 34, 36-37; universal military training, 56; Council veto powers on, 117
Arnold, Matthew, 27
Asia, 34, 124, 143. *See also specific countries*
Asquith, Herbert Henry, first Earl of, 3
Assembly of the League of Nations, first meeting, 13-17, 22-23, 45-46, 126; on treaty reconsideration, 35

Associated Press, 46n, 110
"Association of Nations," 143
Auchincloss, Gordon, 57
Austria, 124, 158; League participation, 53, 126; International Labor Conference and, 64-65, 66, 68

Bailey, Mrs., 25
Baker, Newton D., viii, 54, 72; League modification of Versailles Treaty, 19-24; on universal military training, 56; International Labor Conference and, 67-68; Wilson's illness and, 78; Fosdick resignation and, 106, 108, 109, 116, 119
Baker, Ray Stannard, 46n
Balfour, Arthur James, 3, 36
Balkan States, 26. *See also specific countries*
Baltic, 123
Bankers Trust Company of New York, 39n
banking, 39
Beer, George, 46, 80, 89n
Belgium, 3, 58n, 103, 128, 158; war losses, 19-20; British coal and, 30, 31; Rhine Commission, 36; League Labor Section and, 41n; League of Nations seat and, 66-67, 81-82
Bolivia, 158
Bolling, John Randolph, 138
Bolsheviks, 34
Borah, William Edgar, 69, 96, 116, 117
Brazil, 3, 158
British Civil Service, 23, 38n
British Foreign Office, 3, 24, 65
British War Cabinet, 24
Brussels, Belgium, 66-67, 81-82
Bryan, William Jennings, 110
Buckingham Palace (London), 144
Bulgaria, 57n
Bullitt, William C., vii, 99

159

Index

Index

Index

land mandates and, 36-37; German resumption of trade and, 48-49; Senate reservations and, 49-50, 51-52, 83, 113; shipping lines, 68; League liaison, 112; nationalism and, 116-17; Victory Parade (1919), 144-45

Galileo Galilei, 140, 142
General Education Board, 24n
Geneva, Switzerland, 27, 90, 116, 135, 139; as League of Nations seat, 3, 66-67, 82
Genoa Conference, 136, 139
George V, King of England, 144
Germany, viii, 11, 27, 30, 35, 39; participation in League, 12, 13, 14, 53, 67, 126, 143; demobilization, 20; river control, 20; inflation, 34; Saar Valley and, 35; Sweetser in, 46n; trade resumption, 48-49; League to Enforce Peace in, 60n; International Labor Conference and, 64-65, 66, 67, 68; reparations, 118, 126; Silesian plebiscite, 137n
Gilchrist, Huntington, 18n, 58, 91, 97-98; Senate reservations and, 65, 69, 73; International Labor Conference and, 66, 67-68; Secretariat resignations and, 79, 80, 104, 108-12, 114, 120; on State Department liaison with League, 84-85, 98-100
gold, 15, 33, 126
Great Britain, vii, viii, 137, 138, 158; Foreign Office, 3, 24, 65; League of Nations Secretariat appointments, 3, 103; Council of the League and, 11, 12; war losses, 15, 19-20; civil service, 23, 38n; war cabinet, 24; education and, 26-27; maritime trade, 29; coal, 30-31; American imports, 32; Saar Valley and, 35; Rhine Civilian Commission, 36; International Labor Office and, 38; German trade and, 48-49;

U.S. Senate reservations and, 49, 51, 52, 83, 88, 90, 113; League to Enforce Peace in, 60n; shipping lines, 68; nationalism and, 115, 116-17; London Victory Parade, 144-45
Great Falls (Montana) *Leader*, 135
Great Powers, *see* Allied and Associated Powers
Greece, 3, 26, 87, 158
Gregory, Thomas W., 72
Grey, Edward, 3, 65n, 80, 115; World War I and, 129, 130, 143; Wilson and, 141
Guatemala, 158

Hague, The, 45, 57n, 98
Hague Court of International Justice, 36n, 129. *See also* Permanent Court of International Justice
Haiti, 158
Harbord, James G., 73
Harding, Warren Gamaliel, 126, 131, 133-35
Harvard University, 46n, 47n, 59n
Headlam-Morley, education branch proposal, 24, 27-28
health, 21, 105, 127
Health Convention, 14
Hearst, William Randolph, 115
Hejaz, 134, 158
Herter, Christian A., 59, 60
Hitchcock, Gilbert M., 61, 77, 78
Holt, Hamilton, 60n, 61
Holy Alliance, 12
Honduras, 158
Hoover, Herbert, on international public utilities, 32, 39-40; on Versailles Treaty, 49, 62; League to Enforce Peace and, 61; Fosdick resignation and, 113; election of 1920 and, 115, 134
House, Edward Mandell, 12, 18n, 19, 38, 63; League of Nations Secretariat appointments, 3-4, 5, 70, 71, 79, 80; on League par-

Index

Russia, counterrevolution in, 11; Council representation, 12; Versailles Treaty and, 124, 126, 143

Saar Valley, 10, 19, 20; French military command, 35
Saar Valley Council of Administration of Mines, 42n
Saar Valley Commission, 10, 13, 20
Sadler, Michael, 27
salaries, 4, 29, 103, 135
Salvador, 158
sanitation, 27
Sarajevo, Jugo-Slavia, 22
Savonarola, Girolamo, 140
Scott, James Brown, 98
Secondary Education in Germany (Arnold report), 27
secrecy, *see* public opinion
Secretariat of the League of Nations, appointments, viii-ix, 3-4, 5-6, 17n, 23-24, 46n, 96, 99, 102, 114, 119, 122; League role of, 23-24; International Labor Office and, 41; Establishment Officer, 58n; American resignations from, 62, 70, 71-72, 79-81, 82-83, 96, 102-15, 116, 122, 123-24, 135; Christmas (1919) message, 89-90; Spencer estimate of costs, 91-92
Senate, Versailles Treaty reservations of: Wilson refusal to compromise, ix, 78-79, 85, 91, 95-96, 102, 112, 113-14, 127-29, 141; European view of, 46-54, 55-56, 57, 62-63, 74-75, 76, 83, 113, 122-23, 124-26; political deadlock on, 55-56, 61, 65, 69, 70, 72, 73, 77-79, 80-81, 82, 86-89, 90-92, 93, 94-96, 100, 102, 113-14, 118-19, 120, 121; League Secretariat resignations and, 70-71, 79-81, 103, 108, 110, 112, 114, 119, 120
Senate Foreign Relations Committee, 97, 98
Servia, 26, 27, 57n, 158

Shantung Peninsula, 19, 51, 90
Shepardson, Whitney, 18, 38
Sherman, Lawrence Y., 76
Shotwell, James T., 38
Siam, 158
Silesia, 19, 34, 137, 138
slave trade, 21-22, 87, 127
Smuts, Jan Christiaan, 12, 20
Socrates, 140, 142
South Africa, 12n, 158
South America, 62, 66, 124, 125, 143. *See also specific countries*
Spain, 3, 30, 124, 125, 158
Spencer (Missouri Senator, 1919), 91-92
State Department, United States, 5-6, 18n, 46n; League Secretariat appointments, 4, 85, 96, 114, 120; memorandum (Fosdick, Sweetser, Hudson) on Senate reservations, 54, 57; channels of communications, 57-60, 65, 132; International Labor Conference and, 76, 99; League liaison proposal, 84-85, 98-100; Fosdick analysis of Senate reservations, 86-87; and first meeting of Council, 101-102, 107; Fosdick resignation and, 114; Lansing resignation from, 121; League of Nations communications (1921) and, 132-33, 134
steel strike (1919), 75
Stimson, Henry L., 134
Strauss, 61
strikes, 75
Strong, Benjamin, 38-40
Studies in Diplomatic History (Headlam-Morley), 24n
Sunderland House, London, 18n, 57, 107, 108, 121, 145
Supreme Council, *see* Allied Supreme Council
Sweden, 44, 124, 158
Sweetser, Arthur, 89n, 99, 119; International Labor Office and, 38; memorandum (with Hudson and Fosdick) on Senate res-

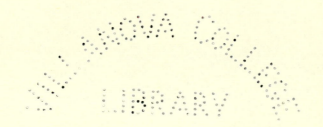